Deep Learning for Computer Vision

Expert techniques to train advanced neural networks using TensorFlow and Keras

Rajalingappaa Shanmugamani

BIRMINGHAM - MUMBAI

Deep Learning for Computer Vision

Commissioning Editor: Amey Varangaonkar
Acquisition Editor: Aman Singh
Content Development Editor: Varun Sony
Technical Editor: Dharmendra Yadav
Copy Editors: Safis Editing
Project Coordinator: Manthan Patel
Proofreader: Safis Editing
Indexer: Pratik Shirodkar
Graphics: Tania Dutta
Production Coordinator: Shantanu Zagade

First published: January 2018

Production reference: 1220118

Published by Packt Publishing Ltd.
Livery Place
35 Livery Street
Birmingham
B3 2PB, UK.

ISBN 978-1-78829-562-8

www.packtpub.com

`mapt.io`

Mapt is an online digital library that gives you full access to over 5,000 books and videos, as well as industry leading tools to help you plan your personal development and advance your career. For more information, please visit our website.

Why subscribe?

- Spend less time learning and more time coding with practical eBooks and Videos from over 4,000 industry professionals

- Improve your learning with Skill Plans built especially for you

- Get a free eBook or video every month

- Mapt is fully searchable

- Copy and paste, print, and bookmark content

PacktPub.com

Did you know that Packt offers eBook versions of every book published, with PDF and ePub files available? You can upgrade to the eBook version at `www.PacktPub.com` and as a print book customer, you are entitled to a discount on the eBook copy. Get in touch with us at `service@packtpub.com` for more details.

At `www.PacktPub.com`, you can also read a collection of free technical articles, sign up for a range of free newsletters, and receive exclusive discounts and offers on Packt books and eBooks.

Foreword

Deep learning is revolutionizing AI, and over the next several decades, it will change the world radically. AI powered by deep learning will be on par in scale with the industrial revolution. This, understandably, has created excitement and fear about the future. But the reality is that just like the industrial revolution and machinery, deep learning will improve industrial capacity and raise the standards of living dramatically for humankind. Rather than replace jobs, it will create many more jobs of a higher stand. This is why this book is so important and timely. Readers of this book will be introduced to deep learning for computer vision, its power, and many applications. This book will give readers a grounding in the fundamentals of an emerging industry that will grow exponentially over the next decade.

Rajalingappaa Shanmugamani is a great researcher whom I have worked with previously on several projects in computer vision. He was the lead engineer in designing and delivering a complex computer vision and deep learning system for fashion search that was deployed in the real world with great success. Among his strengths is his ability to take up state-of-the-art research in complex problems and apply them to real-world situations. He can also break down complex ideas and explain them in simple terms as is demonstrated in this book. Raja is a very ambitious person with great work ethics, and in this book, he has given a great overview of the current state of computer vision using deep learning, a task not many can do in today's industry. This book is a great achievement by Raja and I'm sure the reader will enjoy and benefit from it for many years to come.

Dr. Stephen Moore

Chief Technology Officer, EmotionReader, Singapore

Contributors

About the author

Rajalingappaa Shanmugamani is currently working as a Deep Learning Lead at SAP, Singapore. Previously, he has worked and consulted at various startups for developing computer vision products. He has a Masters from Indian Institute of Technology – Madras where his thesis was based on applications of computer vision in the manufacturing industry. He has published articles in peer-reviewed journals and conferences and applied for few patents in the area of machine learning. In his spare time, he coaches programming and machine learning to school students and engineers.

I thank my spouse Ezhil, family and friends for their immense support. I thank all the teachers, colleagues, managers and mentors from whom I have learned a lot. I thank Jean Ooi for creating the graphics for the book.

About the reviewers

Nishanth Koganti received B.Tech in Electrical Engineering from Indian Institute of Technology Jodhpur, India in 2012, M.E and PhD in Information Science from Nara Institute of Science and Technology, Japan in 2014, 2017 respectively. He is currently a Postdoctoral researcher at the University of Tokyo, Japan. His research interests are in assistive robotics, motor-skills learning, and machine learning. His graduate research was on the development of a clothing assistance robot that helps elderly people to wear clothes.

Packt is searching for authors like you

If you're interested in becoming an author for Packt, please visit `authors.packtpub.com` and apply today. We have worked with thousands of developers and tech professionals, just like you, to help them share their insight with the global tech community. You can make a general application, apply for a specific hot topic that we are recruiting an author for, or submit your own idea.

Table of Contents

Preface

Deep Learning for Computer Vision is a book intended for readers who want to learn deep-learning-based computer vision techniques for various applications. This book will give the reader tools and techniques to develop computer-vision-based products. There are plenty of practical examples covered in the book to follow the theory.

Who this book is for

The reader wants to know how to apply deep learning to computer vision problems such as classification, detection, retrieval, segmentation, generation, captioning, and video classification. The reader also wants to understand how to achieve good accuracy under various constraints such as less data, imbalanced classes, and noise. Then the reader also wants to know how to deploy trained models on various platforms (AWS, Google Cloud, Raspberry Pi, and mobile phones). After completing this book, the reader should be able to develop code for problems of person detection, face recognition, product search, medical image segmentation, image generation, image captioning, video classification, and so on.

What this book covers

Chapter 1, *Getting Started*, introduces the basics of deep learning and makes the readers familiar with the vocabulary. The readers will install the software packages necessary to follow the rest of the chapters.

Chapter 2, *Image Classification*, talks about the image classification problem, which is labeling an image as a whole. The readers will learn about image classification techniques and train a deep learning model for pet classification. They will also learn methods to improve accuracy and dive deep into variously advanced architectures.

Chapter 3, *Image Retrieval*, covers deep features and image retrieval. The reader will learn about various methods of obtaining model visualization, visual features, inference using TensorFlow, and serving and using visual features for product retrieval.

Chapter 4, *Object Detection*, talks about detecting objects in images. The reader will learn about various techniques of object detection and apply them for pedestrian detection. The TensorFlow API for object detection will be utilized in this chapter.

Chapter 5, *Semantic Segmentation*, covers segmenting of images pixel-wise. The readers will earn about segmentation techniques and train a model for segmentation of medical images.

Chapter 6, *Similarity Learning*, talks about similarity learning. The readers will learn about similarity matching and how to train models for face recognition. A model to train facial landmark is illustrated.

Chapter 7, *Image Captioning*, is about generating or selecting captions for images. The readers will learn natural language processing techniques and how to generate captions for images using those techniques.

Chapter 8, *Generative Models*, talks about generating synthetic images for various purposes. The readers will learn what generative models are and use them for image generation applications, such as style transfer, training data, and so on.

Chapter 9, *Video Classification*, covers computer vision techniques for video data. The readers will understand the key differences between solving video versus image problems and implement video classification techniques.

Chapter 10, *Deployment*, talks about the deployment steps for deep learning models. The reader will learn how to deploy trained models and optimize for speed on various platforms.

To get the most out of this book

The examples covered in this book can be run with Windows, Ubuntu, or Mac. All the installation instructions are covered. Basic knowledge of Python and machine learning is required. It's preferable that the reader has GPU hardware but it's not necessary.

Download the example code files

You can download the example code files for this book from your account at www.packtpub.com. If you purchased this book elsewhere, you can visit www.packtpub.com/support and register to have the files emailed directly to you.

You can download the code files by following these steps:

1. Log in or register at www.packtpub.com.
2. Select the **SUPPORT** tab.
3. Click on **Code Downloads & Errata**.
4. Enter the name of the book in the **Search** box and follow the onscreen instructions.

Once the file is downloaded, please make sure that you unzip or extract the folder using the latest version of:

- WinRAR/7-Zip for Windows
- Zipeg/iZip/UnRarX for Mac
- 7-Zip/PeaZip for Linux

The code bundle for the book is also hosted on GitHub at https://github.com/PacktPublishing/Deep-Learning-for-Computer-Vision. We also have other code bundles from our rich catalog of books and videos available at https://github.com/PacktPublishing/. Check them out!

Conventions used

There are a number of text conventions used throughout this book.

CodeInText: Indicates code words in text, database table names, folder names, filenames, file extensions, pathnames, dummy URLs, user input, and Twitter handles. Here is an example: "Note that the graph is written once with the summary_writer."

A block of code is set as follows:

```
merged_summary_operation = tf.summary.merge_all()
train_summary_writer = tf.summary.FileWriter('/tmp/train', session.graph)
test_summary_writer = tf.summary.FileWriter('/tmp/test')
```

Any command-line input or output is written as follows:

```
wget http://www.robots.ox.ac.uk/~vgg/data/pets/data/images.tar.gz
wget http://www.robots.ox.ac.uk/~vgg/data/pets/data/annotations.tar.gz
```

Bold: Indicates a new term, an important word, or words that you see onscreen. For example, words in menus or dialog boxes appear in the text like this. Here is an example: "Once you are done, terminate the instance by clicking **Actions | Instance State | Terminat**."

 Warnings or important notes appear like this.

 Tips and tricks appear like this.

Get in touch

Feedback from our readers is always welcome.

General feedback: Email `feedback@packtpub.com` and mention the book title in the subject of your message. If you have questions about any aspect of this book, please email us at `questions@packtpub.com`.

Errata: Although we have taken every care to ensure the accuracy of our content, mistakes do happen. If you have found a mistake in this book, we would be grateful if you would report this to us. Please visit `www.packtpub.com/submit-errata`, selecting your book, clicking on the Errata Submission Form link, and entering the details.

Piracy: If you come across any illegal copies of our works in any form on the Internet, we would be grateful if you would provide us with the location address or website name. Please contact us at `copyright@packtpub.com` with a link to the material.

If you are interested in becoming an author: If there is a topic that you have expertise in and you are interested in either writing or contributing to a book, please visit `authors.packtpub.com`.

Reviews

Please leave a review. Once you have read and used this book, why not leave a review on the site that you purchased it from? Potential readers can then see and use your unbiased opinion to make purchase decisions, we at Packt can understand what you think about our products, and our authors can see your feedback on their book. Thank you!

For more information about Packt, please visit packtpub.com.

1
Getting Started

Computer vision is the science of understanding or manipulating images and videos. Computer vision has a lot of applications, including autonomous driving, industrial inspection, and augmented reality. The use of deep learning for computer vision can be categorized into multiple categories: classification, detection, segmentation, and generation, both in images and videos. In this book, you will learn how to train deep learning models for computer vision applications and deploy them on multiple platforms. We will use **TensorFlow**, a popular python library for deep learning throughout this book for the examples. In this chapter, we will cover the following topics:

- The basics and vocabulary of deep learning
- How deep learning meets computer vision?
- Setting up the development environment that will be used for the examples covered in this book
- Getting a feel for TensorFlow, along with its powerful tools, such as TensorBoard and TensorFlow Serving

Understanding deep learning

Computer vision as a field has a long history. With the emergence of deep learning, computer vision has proven to be useful for various applications. Deep learning is a collection of techniques from **artificial neural network (ANN)**, which is a branch of machine learning. ANNs are modelled on the human brain; there are nodes linked to each other that pass information to each other. In the following sections, we will discuss in detail how deep learning works by understanding the commonly used basic terms.

Perceptron

An artificial neuron or perceptron takes several inputs and performs a weighted summation to produce an output. The weight of the perceptron is determined during the training process and is based on the training data. The following is a diagram of the perceptron:

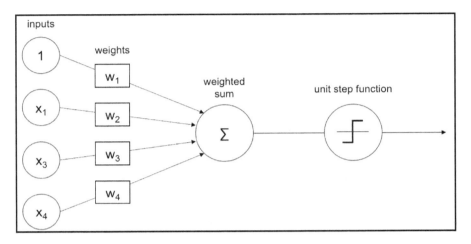

The inputs are weighted and summed as shown in the preceding image. The sum is then passed through a unit step function, in this case, for a binary classification problem. A perceptron can only learn simple functions by learning the weights from examples. The process of learning the weights is called training. The training on a perceptron can be done through gradient-based methods which are explained in a later section. The output of the perceptron can be passed through an `activation` function or `transfer` function, which will be explained in the next section.

Activation functions

The `activation` functions make **neural nets** nonlinear. An activation function decides whether a perceptron should fire or not. During training activation, functions play an important role in adjusting the gradients. An `activation` function such as sigmoid, shown in the next section, attenuates the values with higher magnitudes. This nonlinear behaviour of the `activation` function gives the deep nets to learn complex functions. Most of the `activation` functions are continuous and differential functions, except rectified unit at 0. A continuous function has small changes in output for every small change in input. A differential function has a derivative existing at every point in the domain.

In order to train a neural network, the function has to be differentiable. Following are a few `activation` functions.

Don't worry if you don't understand the terms like continuous and differentiable in detail. It will become clearer over the chapters.

Sigmoid

Sigmoid can be considered a smoothened step function and hence differentiable. Sigmoid is useful for converting any value to probabilities and can be used for binary classification. The sigmoid maps input to a value in the range of 0 to 1, as shown in the following graph:

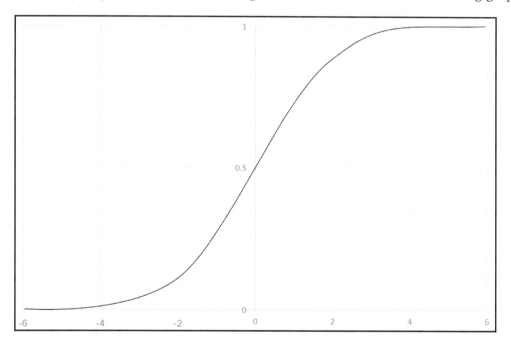

The change in Y values with respect to X is going to be small, and hence, there will be vanishing gradients. After some learning, the change may be small. Another activation function called `tanh`, explained in next section, is a scaled version of sigmoid and avoids the problem of a vanishing gradient.

The hyperbolic tangent function

The hyperbolic tangent function, or `tanh`, is the scaled version of sigmoid. Like sigmoid, it is smooth and differentiable. The `tanh` maps input to a value in the range of -1 to 1, as shown in the following graph:

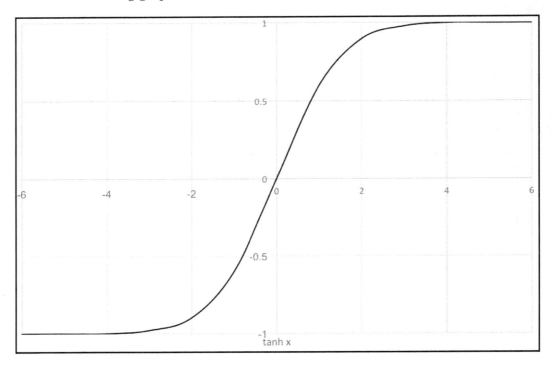

The gradients are more stable than sigmoid and hence have fewer vanishing gradient problems. Both sigmoid and `tanh` fire all the time, making the ANN really heavy. The **Rectified Linear Unit (ReLU)** activation function, explained in the next section, avoids this pitfall by not firing at times.

The Rectified Linear Unit (ReLU)

ReLu can let big numbers pass through. This makes a few neurons stale and they don't fire. This increases the sparsity, and hence, it is good. The `ReLU` maps input x to max $(0, x)$, that is, they map negative inputs to 0, and positive inputs are output without any change as shown in the following graph:

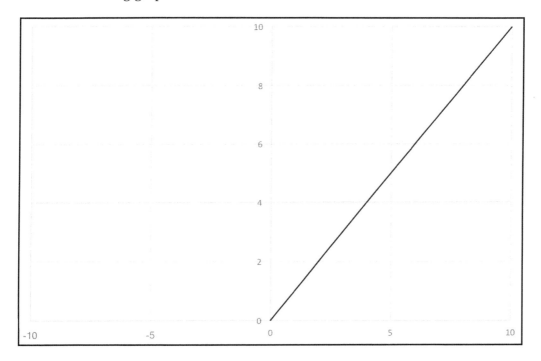

Because ReLU doesn't fire all the time, it can be trained faster. Since the function is simple, it is computationally the least expensive. Choosing the `activation` function is very dependent on the application. Nevertheless, ReLU works well for a large range of problems. In the next section, you will learn how to stack several perceptrons together that can learn more complex functions than perceptron.

Artificial neural network (ANN)

ANN is a collection of perceptrons and `activation` functions. The perceptrons are connected to form hidden layers or units. The hidden units form the nonlinear basis that maps the input layers to output layers in a lower-dimensional space, which is also called artificial neural networks. ANN is a map from input to output. The map is computed by weighted addition of the inputs with biases. The values of weight and bias values along with the architecture are called `model`.

The training process determines the values of these weights and biases. The model values are initialized with random values during the beginning of the training. The error is computed using a loss function by contrasting it with the ground truth. Based on the loss computed, the weights are tuned at every step. The training is stopped when the error cannot be further reduced. The training process learns the features during the training. The features are a better representation than the raw images. The following is a diagram of an artificial neural network, or multi-layer perceptron:

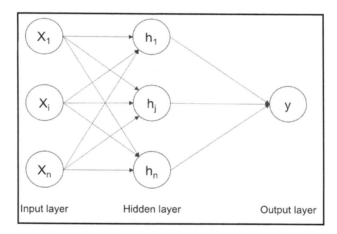

Several inputs of x are passed through a hidden layer of perceptrons and summed to the output. The universal approximation theorem suggests that such a neural network can approximate any function. The hidden layer can also be called a dense layer. Every layer can have one of the `activation` functions described in the previous section. The number of hidden layers and perceptrons can be chosen based on the problem. There are a few more things that make this multilayer perceptron work for multi-class classification problems. A multi-class classification problem tries to discriminate more than ten categories. We will explore those terms in the following sections.

One-hot encoding

One-hot encoding is a way to represent the target variables or classes in case of a classification problem. The target variables can be converted from the string labels to one-hot encoded vectors. A one-hot vector is filled with *1* at the index of the target class but with *0* everywhere else. For example, if the target classes are cat and dog, they can be represented by [*1, 0*] and [*0, 1*], respectively. For 1,000 classes, one-hot vectors will be of size 1,000 integers with all zeros but *1*. It makes no assumptions about the similarity of target variables. With the combination of one-hot encoding with softmax explained in the following section, multi-class classification becomes possible in ANN.

Softmax

Softmax is a way of forcing the neural networks to output the sum of 1. Thereby, the output values of the `softmax` function can be considered as part of a probability distribution. This is useful in multi-class classification problems. Softmax is a kind of `activation` function with the speciality of output summing to 1. It converts the outputs to probabilities by dividing the output by summation of all the other values. The Euclidean distance can be computed between softmax probabilities and one-hot encoding for optimization. But the cross-entropy explained in the next section is a better cost function to optimize.

Cross-entropy

Cross-entropy compares the distance between the outputs of softmax and one-hot encoding. Cross-entropy is a loss function for which error has to be minimized. Neural networks estimate the probability of the given data to every class. The probability has to be maximized to the correct target label. Cross-entropy is the summation of negative logarithmic probabilities. Logarithmic value is used for numerical stability. Maximizing a function is equivalent to minimizing the negative of the same function. In the next section, we will see the following regularization methods to avoid the overfitting of ANN:

- Dropout
- Batch normalization
- L1 and L2 normalization

Dropout

Dropout is an effective way of regularizing neural networks to avoid the overfitting of ANN. During training, the dropout layer cripples the neural network by removing hidden units stochastically as shown in the following image:

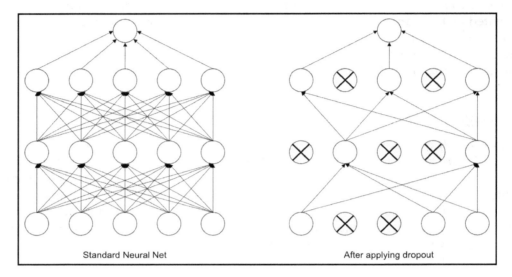

Note how the neurons are randomly trained. Dropout is also an efficient way of combining several neural networks. For each training case, we randomly select a few hidden units so that we end up with different architectures for each case. This is an extreme case of bagging and model averaging. Dropout layer should not be used during the inference as it is not necessary.

Batch normalization

Batch normalization, or batch-norm, increase the stability and performance of neural network training. It normalizes the output from a layer with zero mean and a standard deviation of 1. This reduces overfitting and makes the network train faster. It is very useful in training complex neural networks.

L1 and L2 regularization

L1 penalizes the absolute value of the weight and tends to make the weights zero. L2 penalizes the squared value of the weight and tends to make the weight smaller during the training. Both the regularizes assume that models with smaller weights are better.

Training neural networks

Training ANN is tricky as it contains several parameters to optimize. The procedure of updating the weights is called backpropagation. The procedure to minimize the error is called optimization. We will cover both of them in detail in the next sections.

Backpropagation

A backpropagation algorithm is commonly used for training artificial neural networks. The weights are updated from backward based on the error calculated as shown in the following image:

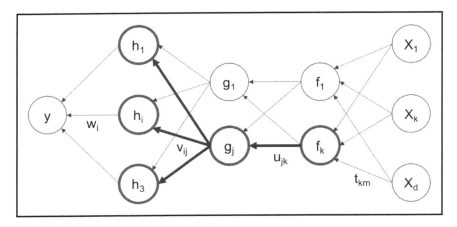

After calculating the error, gradient descent can be used to calculate the weight updating, as explained in the next section.

Gradient descent

The gradient descent algorithm performs multidimensional optimization. The objective is to reach the global maximum. Gradient descent is a popular optimization technique used in many machine-learning models. It is used to improve or optimize the model prediction. One implementation of gradient descent is called the **stochastic gradient descent** (**SGD**) and is becoming more popular (explained in the next section) in neural networks. Optimization involves calculating the error value and changing the weights to achieve that minimal error. The direction of finding the minimum is the negative of the gradient of the loss function. The gradient descent procedure is qualitatively shown in the following figure:

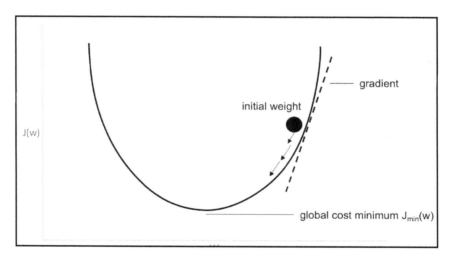

The learning rate determines how big each step should be. Note that the ANN with nonlinear activations will have local minima. SGD works better in practice for optimizing non-convex cost functions.

Stochastic gradient descent

SGD is the same as gradient descent, except that it is used for only partial data to train every time. The parameter is called mini-batch size. Theoretically, even one example can be used for training. In practice, it is better to experiment with various numbers. In the next section, we will discuss convolutional neural networks that work better on image data than the standard ANN.

Visit `https://yihui.name/animation/example/grad-desc/` to see a great visualization of gradient descent on convex and non-convex surfaces.

Playing with TensorFlow playground

TensorFlow playground is an interactive visualization of neural networks. Visit `http://playground.tensorflow.org/`, play by changing the parameters to see how the previously mentioned terms work together. Here is a screenshot of the playground:

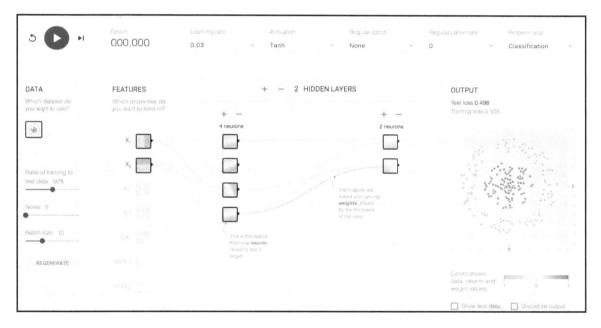

Dashboard in the TensorFlow playground

As shown previously, the reader can change learning rate, activation, regularization, hidden units, and layers to see how it affects the training process. You can spend some time adjusting the parameters to get the intuition of how neural networks for various kinds of data.

Convolutional neural network

Convolutional neural networks (**CNN**) are similar to the neural networks described in the previous sections. CNNs have weights, biases, and outputs through a nonlinear activation. Regular neural networks take inputs and the neurons fully connected to the next layers. Neurons within the same layer don't share any connections. If we use regular neural networks for images, they will be very large in size due to a huge number of neurons, resulting in overfitting. We cannot use this for images, as images are large in size. Increase the model size as it requires a huge number of neurons. An image can be considered a volume with dimensions of height, width, and depth. Depth is the channel of an image, which is red, blue, and green. The neurons of a CNN are arranged in a volumetric fashion to take advantage of the volume. Each of the layers transforms the input volume to an output volume as shown in the following image:

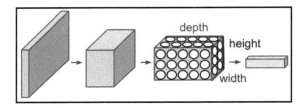

Convolution neural network filters encode by transformation. The learned filters detect features or patterns in images. The deeper the layer, the more abstract the pattern is. Some analyses have shown that these layers have the ability to detect edges, corners, and patterns. The learnable parameters in CNN layers are less than the dense layer described in the previous section.

Kernel

Kernel is the parameter convolution layer used to convolve the image. The convolution operation is shown in the following figure:

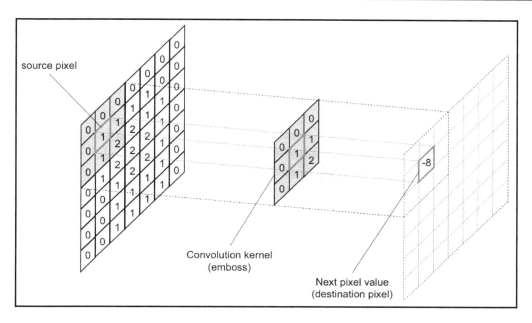

source pixel

Convolution kernel
(emboss)

Next pixel value
(destination pixel)

The kernel has two parameters, called stride and size. The size can be any dimension of a rectangle. Stride is the number of pixels moved every time. A stride of length 1 produces an image of almost the same size, and a stride of length 2 produces half the size. Padding the image will help in achieving the same size of the input.

Max pooling

Pooling layers are placed between convolution layers. Pooling layers reduce the size of the image across layers by sampling. The sampling is done by selecting the maximum value in a window. Average pooling averages over the window. Pooling also acts as a regularization technique to avoid overfitting. Pooling is carried out on all the channels of features. Pooling can also be performed with various strides.

The size of the window is a measure of the receptive field of CNN. The following figure shows an example of max pooling:

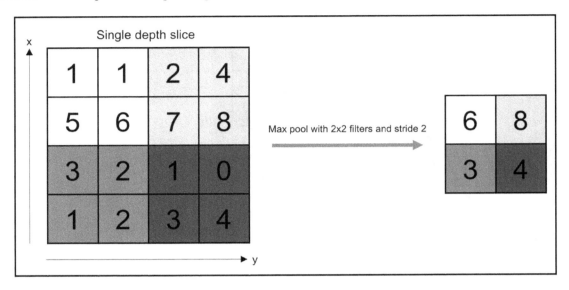

CNN is the single most important component of any deep learning model for computer vision. It won't be an exaggeration to state that it will be impossible for any computer to have vision without a CNN. In the next sections, we will discuss a couple of advanced layers that can be used for a few applications.

 Visit https://www.youtube.com/watch?v=jajksuQW4mc for a great visualization of a CNN and max-pooling operation.

Recurrent neural networks (RNN)

Recurrent neural networks (RNN) can model sequential information. They do not assume that the data points are intensive. They perform the same task from the output of the previous data of a series of sequence data. This can also be thought of as memory. RNN cannot remember from longer sequences or time. It is unfolded during the training process, as shown in the following image:

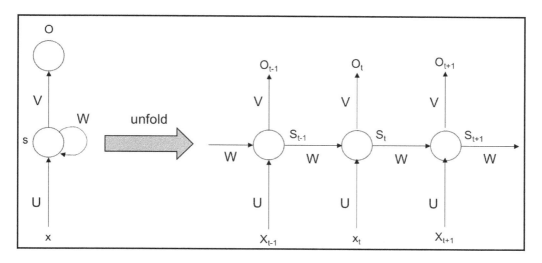

As shown in the preceding figure, the step is unfolded and trained each time. During backpropagation, the gradients can vanish over time. To overcome this problem, Long short-term memory can be used to remember over a longer time period.

Long short-term memory (LSTM)

Long short-term memory (**LSTM**) can store information for longer periods of time, and hence, it is efficient in capturing long-term efficiencies. The following figure illustrates how an LSTM cell is designed:

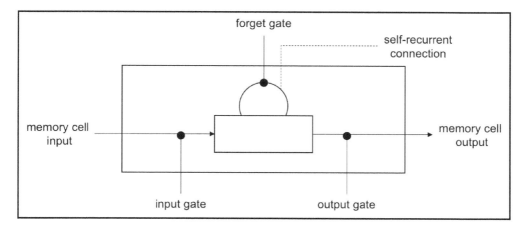

LSTM has several gates: forget, input, and output. Forget gate maintains the information previous state. The input gate updates the current state using the input. The output gate decides the information be passed to the next state. The ability to forget and retain only the important things enables LSTM to remember over a longer time period. You have learned the deep learning vocabulary that will be used throughout the book. In the next section, we will see how deep learning can be used in the context of computer vision.

Deep learning for computer vision

Computer vision enables the properties of human vision on a computer. A computer could be in the form of a smartphone, drones, CCTV, MRI scanner, and so on, with various sensors for perception. The sensor produces images in a digital form that has to be interpreted by the computer. The basic building block of such interpretation or intelligence is explained in the next section. The different problems that arise in computer vision can be effectively solved using deep learning techniques.

Classification

Image classification is the task of labelling the whole image with an object or concept with confidence. The applications include gender classification given an image of a person's face, identifying the type of pet, tagging photos, and so on. The following is an output of such a classification task:

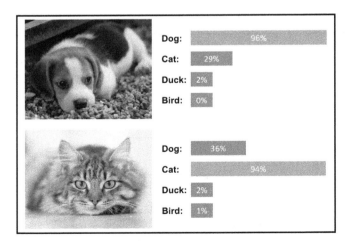

The Chapter 2, *Image Classification*, covers in detail the methods that can be used for classification tasks and in Chapter 3, *Image Retrieval*, we use the classification models for visualization of deep learning models and retrieve similar images.

Detection or localization and segmentation

Detection or localization is a task that finds an object in an image and localizes the object with a bounding box. This task has many applications, such as finding pedestrians and signboards for self-driving vehicles. The following image is an illustration of detection:

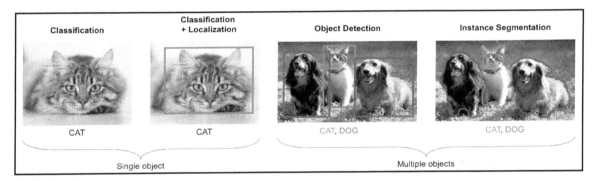

Segmentation is the task of doing pixel-wise classification. This gives a fine separation of objects. It is useful for processing medical images and satellite imagery. More examples and explanations can be found in Chapter 4, Object Detection and Chapter 5, *Image Segmentation*.

Similarity learning

Similarity learning is the process of learning how two images are similar. A score can be computed between two images based on the semantic meaning as shown in the following image:

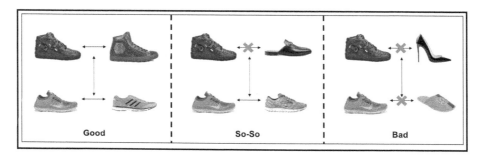

There are several applications of this, from finding similar products to performing the facial identification. Chapter 6, *Similarity learning*, deals with similarity learning techniques.

Image captioning

Image captioning is the task of describing the image with text as shown [below] here:

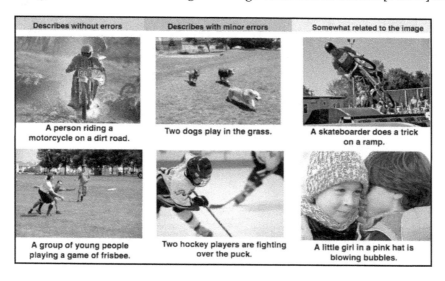

Reproduced with permission from Vinyals et al.

The `Chapter 8`, *Image Captioning*, goes into detail about image captioning. This is a unique case where techniques of **natural language processing** (**NLP**) and computer vision have to be combined.

Generative models

Generative models are very interesting as they generate images. The following is an example of style transfer application where an image is generated with the content of that image and style of other images:

Reproduced with permission from Gatys et al.

Images can be generated for other purposes such as new training examples, super-resolution images, and so on. The Chapter 7, *Generative Models*, goes into detail of generative models.

Video analysis

Video analysis processes a video as a whole, as opposed to images as in previous cases. It has several applications, such as sports tracking, intrusion detection, and surveillance cameras. Chapter 9, *Video Classification*, deals with video-specific applications. The new dimension of temporal data gives rise to lots of interesting applications. In the next section, we will see how to set up the development environment.

Development environment setup

In this section, we will set up the programming environment that will be useful for following the examples in the rest of the book. Readers may have the following choices of Operating Systems:

- **Development Operating Systems(OS)** such as Mac, Ubuntu, or Windows
- **Deployment Operating Systems** such as Mac, Windows, Android, iOs, or Ubuntu installed in Cloud platform such as **Amazon Web Services (AWS)**, **Google Cloud Platform (GCP)**, Azure, Tegra, Raspberry Pi

Irrespective of the platforms, all the code developed in this book should run without any issues. In this chapter, we will cover the installation procedures for the development environment. In Chapter 10, *Deployment*, we will cover installation for deployment in various other environments, such as AWS, GCP, Azure, Tegra, and Raspberry Pi.

Hardware and Operating Systems - OS

For the development environment, you need to have a lot of computing power as training is significantly computationally expensive. Mac users are rather limited to computing power. Windows and Ubuntu users can beef up their development environment with more processors and **General Purpose - Graphics Processing Unit (GP-GPU)**, which will be explained in the next section.

General Purpose - Graphics Processing Unit (GP-GPU)

GP-GPUs are special hardware that speeds up the training process of training deep learning models. The GP-GPUs supplied by NVIDIA company are very popular for deep learning training and deployment as it has well-matured software and community support. Readers can set up a machine with such a GP-GPU for faster training. There are plenty of choices available, and the reader can choose one based on budget. It is also important to choose the RAM, CPU, and hard disk corresponding to the power of the GP-GPU. After the installation of the hardware, the following drivers and libraries have to be installed. Readers who are using Mac, or using Windows/Ubuntu without a GP-GPU, can skip the installation.

The following are the libraries that are required for setting up the environment:

- **Computer Unified Device Architecture (CUDA)**
- **CUDA Deep Neural Network (CUDNN)**

Computer Unified Device Architecture - CUDA

CUDA is the API layer provided by NVIDIA, using the parallel nature of the GPU. When this is installed, drivers for the hardware are also installed. First, download the CUDA library from the NVIDIA-portal: `https://developer.nvidia.com/cuda-downloads`.

Go through the instructions on the page, download the driver, and follow the installation instructions. Here is the screenshot of Ubuntu CUDA and the installation instructions:

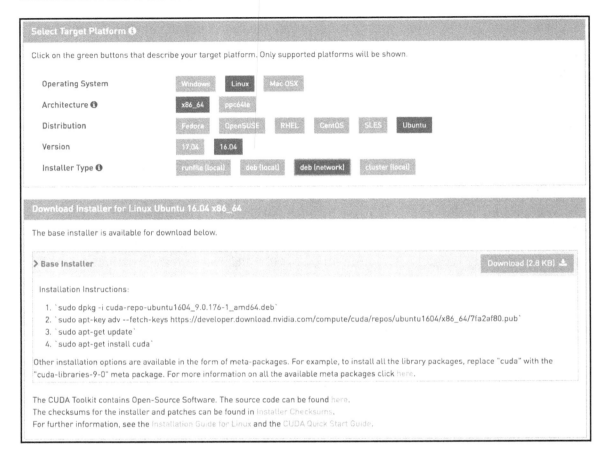

These commands would have installed the `cuda-drivers` and the other CUDA APIs required.

You can check whether the drivers are properly installed by typing `nvidia-smi` in the command prompt.

CUDA Deep Neural Network - CUDNN

The CUDNN library provides primitives for deep learning algorithms. Since this package is provided by NVIDIA, it is highly optimized for their hardware and runs faster. Several standard routines for deep learning are provided in this package. These packages are used by famous deep learning libraries such as tensorflow, caffe, and so on. In the next section, instructions are provided for installing CUDNN. You can download CUDNN from the NVIDIA portal at https://developer.nvidia.com/rdp/cudnn-download.

 User account is required (free signup).

Copy the relevant files to the CUDA folders, making them faster to run on GPUs. We will not use CUDA and CUDNN libraries directly. Tensorflow uses these to work on GP-GPU with optimized routines.

Installing software packages

There are several libraries required for trained deep learning models. We will install the following libraries and see the reason for selecting the following packages over the competing packages:

- Python and other dependencies
- OpenCV
- TensorFlow
- Keras

Python

Python is the de-facto choice for any data science application. It has the largest community and support ecosystem of libraries. TensorFlow API for Python is the most complete, and hence, Python is the natural language of choice. Python has two versions—Python2.x and Python3.x. In this book, we will discuss Python3.x. There are several reasons for this choice:

- Python 2.x development will be stopped by 2020, and hence, Python3.x is the future of Python

- Python 3.x avoids many design flaws in the original implementation
- Contrary to popular belief, Python3.x has as many supporting libraries for data science as Python 2.x.

We will use Python version 3 throughout this book. Go to `https://www.python.org/downloads/` and download version 3 according to the OS. Install Python by following the steps given in the download link. After installing Python, **pip3** has to be installed for easy installation of Python packages. Then install the several Python packages by entering the following command, so that you can install `OpenCV` and `tensorflow` later:

```
sudo pip3 install numpy scipy scikit-learn pillow h5py
```

The description of the preceding installed packages is given as follows:

- `numpy` is a highly-optimized numerical computation package. It has a powerful N-dimensional package array object, and the matrix operations of `numpy` library are highly optimized for speed. An image can be stored as a 3-dimensional `numpy` object.
- `scipy` has several routines for scientific and engineering calculations. We will use some optimization packages later in the book.
- `scikit-learn` is a machine-learning library from which we will use many helper functions.
- `Ppillow` is useful for image loading and basic operations.
- `H5py` package is a Pythonic interface to the HDF5 binary data format. This is the format to store models trained using Keras.

Open Computer Vision - OpenCV

The `OpenCV` is a famous computer vision library. There are several image processing routines available in this library that can be of great use. Following is the step of installing OpenCV in Ubuntu.

```
sudo apt-get install python-opencv
```

Similar steps can be found for other OSes at `https://opencv.org/`. It is cross-platform and optimized for CPU-intensive applications. It has interfaces for several programming languages and is supported by Windows, Ubuntu, and Mac.

The TensorFlow library

The `tensorflow` is an open source library for the development and deployment of deep learning models. TensorFlow uses computational graphs for data flow and numerical computations. In other words, data, or tensor, flows through the graph, thus the name `tensorflow`. The graph has nodes that enable any numerical computation and, hence, are suitable for deep learning operations. It provides a single API for all kinds of platforms and hardware. TensorFlow handles all the complexity of scaling and optimization at the backend. It was originally developed for research at Google. It is the most famous deep learning library, with a large community and comes with tools for visualization and deployment in production.

Installing TensorFlow

Install `tensorflow` using pip3 for the CPU using the following command:

```
sudo pip3 install tensorflow
```

If you are using GPU hardware and have installed CUDA and CUDNN, install the GPU version of the `tensorflow` with the following command:

```
sudo pip3 install tensorflow-gpu
```

Now the `tensorflow` is installed and ready for use. We will try out a couple of examples to understand how TensorFlow works.

TensorFlow example to print Hello, TensorFlow

We will do an example using TensorFlow directly in the Python shell. In this example, we will print **Hello, TensorFlow** using TensorFlow.

1. Invoke Python from your shell by typing the following in the command prompt:

   ```
   python3
   ```

2. Import the `tensorflow` library by entering the following command:

   ```
   >>> import tensorflow as tf
   ```

3. Next, define a constant with the string `Hello, TensorFlow`. This is different from the usual Python assignment operations as the value is not yet initialized:

```
>>> hello = tf.constant('Hello, TensorFlow!')
```

4. Create a session to initialize the computational graph, and give a name to the session:

```
>>> session = tf.Session()
```

The session can be run with the variable `hello` as the parameter.

5. Now the graph executes and returns that particular variable that is printed:

```
>>> print(session.run(hello))
```

It should print the following:

```
Hello, TensorFlow!
```

Let us look at one more example to understand how the session and graph work.

Visit `https://github.com/rajacheers/DeepLearningForComputerVision` to get the code for all the examples presented in the book. The code will be organised according to chapters. You can raise issues and get help in the repository.

TensorFlow example for adding two numbers

Here is another simple example of how TensorFlow is used to add two numbers.

1. Create a Python file and import `tensorflow` using the following code:

```
import tensorflow as tf
```

The preceding import will be necessary for all the latter examples. It is assumed that the reader has imported the library for all the examples. A `placeholder` can be defined in the following manner. The placeholders are not loaded when assigned. Here, a variable is defined as a `placeholder` with a type of `float32`. A `placeholder` is an empty declaration and can take values when a session is run.

2. Now we define a `placeholder` as shown in the following code:

```
x = tf.placeholder(tf.float32)
y = tf.placeholder(tf.float32)
```

3. Now the sum operation of the placeholders can be defined as a usual addition. Here, the operation is not executed but just defined using the following code:

```
z = x + y
```

4. The session can be created as shown in the previous example. The graph is ready for executing the computations when defined as shown below:

```
session = tf.Session()
```

5. Define the value of the `placeholder` in a dictionary format:

```
values = {x: 5.0, y: 4.0}
```

6. Run the session with variable `c` and the values. The graph feeds the values to appropriate placeholders and gets the value back for variable `c`:

```
result = session.run([z], values)
print(result)
```

This program should print [**9.0**] as the result of the addition.

It's understandable that this is not the best way to add two numbers. This example is to understand how tensors and operations are defined in TensorFlow. Imagine how difficult it will be to use a trillion numbers and add them. TensorFlow enables that scale with ease with the same APIs. In the next section, we will see how to install and use TensorBoard and TensorFlow serving.

TensorBoard

TensorBoard is a suite of visualization tools for training deep learning-based models with TensorFlow. The following data can be visualized in TensorBoard:

- **Graphs**: Computation graphs, device placements, and tensor details
- **Scalars**: Metrics such as loss, accuracy over iterations
- **Images**: Used to see the images with corresponding labels

- **Audio**: Used to listen to audio from training or a generated one
- **Distribution**: Used to see the distribution of some scalar
- **Histograms**: Includes histogram of weights and biases
- **Projector**: Helps visualize the data in 3-dimensional space
- **Text**: Prints the training text data
- **Profile**: Sees the hardware resources utilized for training

Tensorboard is installed along with TensorFlow. Go to the python3 prompt and type the following command, similar to the previous example, to start using Tensorboard:

```
x = tf.placeholder(tf.float32, name='x')
y = tf.placeholder(tf.float32, name='y')
z = tf.add(x, y, name='sum')
```

Note that an argument name has been provided as an extra parameter to placeholders and operations. These are names that can be seen when we visualize the graph. Now we can write the graph to a specific folder with the following command in TensorBoard:

```
session = tf.Session()
summary_writer = tf.summary.FileWriter('/tmp/1', session.graph)
```

This command writes the graph to disk to a particular folder given in the argument. Now Tensorboard can be invoked with the following command:

```
tensorboard --logdir=/tmp/1
```

Any directory can be passed as an argument for the logdir option where the files are stored. Go to a browser and paste the following URL to start the visualization to access the TensorBoard:

```
http://localhost:6006/
```

The browser should display something like this:

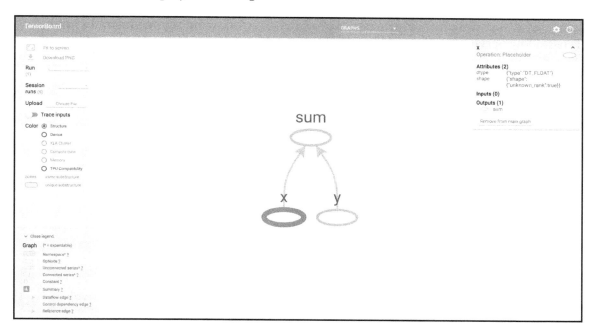

The TensorBoard visualization in the browser window

The graph of addition is displayed with the names given for the placeholders. When we click on them, we can see all the particulars of the tensor for that operation on the right side. Make yourself familiar with the tabs and options. There are several parts in this window. We will learn about them in different chapters. TensorBoard is one the best distinguishing tools in TensorFlow, which makes it better than any other deep learning framework.

The TensorFlow Serving tool

TensorFlow Serving is a tool in TensorFlow developed for deployment environments that are flexible, providing high latency and throughput environments. Any deep learning model trained with TensorFlow can be deployed with serving. Install the Serving by running the following command:

```
sudo apt-get install tensorflow-model-server
```

Step-by-step instructions on how to use serving will be described in `Chapter 3`, *Image Retrieval*. Note that the Serving is easy to install only in Ubuntu; for other OSes, please refer to `https://www.tensorflow.org/serving/setup`. The following figure illustrates how TensorFlow Serving and TensorFlow interact in production environments:

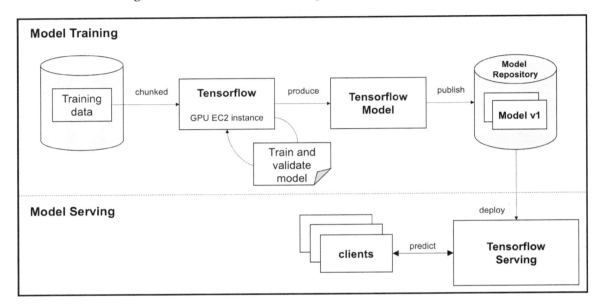

Many models can be produced by the training process, and Serving takes care of switching them seamlessly without any downtime. TensorFlow Serving is not required for all the following chapters, except for `Chapter 3`, *Image Retrieval* and `Chapter 10`, *Deployment*.

The Keras library

`Keras` is an open source library for deep learning written in Python. It provides an easy interface to use TensorFlow as a backend. Keras can also be used with Theano, deep learning 4j, or CNTK as its backend. Keras is designed for easy and fast experimentation by focusing on friendliness, modularity, and extensibility. It is a self-contained framework and runs seamlessly between CPU and GPU. Keras can be installed separately or used within TensorFlow itself using the `tf.keras` API. In this book, we will use the `tf.keras` API. We have seen the steps to install the required libraries for the development environment. Having CUDA, CUDNN, OpenCV, TensorFlow, and Keras installed and running smoothly is vital for the following chapters.

Summary

In this chapter, we have covered the basics of deep learning. The vocabulary introduced in this chapter will be used throughout this book, hence, you can refer back to this chapter often. The applications of computer vision are also shown with examples. Installations of all the software packages for various platforms for the development environment were also covered.

In the next chapter, we will discuss how to train classification models using both Keras and TensorFlow on a dataset. We will look at how to improve the accuracy using a bigger model and other techniques such as augmentation, and fine-tuning. Then, we will see several advanced models proposed by several people around the world, achieving the best accuracy in competitions.

2
Image Classification

Image classification is the task of classifying a whole image as a single label. For example, an image classification task could label an image as a dog or a cat, given an image is either a dog or a cat. In this chapter, we will see how to use TensorFlow to build such an image classification model and also learn the techniques to improve the accuracy.

We will cover the following topics in this chapter:

- Training the MNIST model in TensorFlow
- Training the MNIST model in Keras
- Other popular image testing datasets
- The bigger deep learning models
- Training a model for cats versus dogs
- Developing real-world applications

Training the MNIST model in TensorFlow

In this section, we will learn about the **Modified National Institute of Standards and Technology (MNIST)** database data and build a simple classification model. The objective of this section is to learn the general framework for deep learning and use TensorFlow for the same. First, we will build a perceptron or logistic regression model. Then, we will train a CNN to achieve better accuracy. We will also see how TensorBoard helps visualize the training process and understand the parameters.

The MNIST datasets

The MNIST data has handwritten digits from 0–9 with 60,000 images for training and 10,000 images for testing. This database is widely used to try algorithms with minimum preprocessing. It's a good and compact database to learn machine learning algorithms. This is the most famous database for image classification problems. A few examples are shown here:

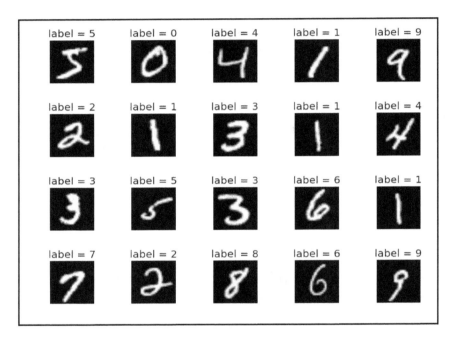

As can be seen in the preceding figure, there are 10 labels for these handwritten characters. The images are normalized to the size of 28 image pixels by 28 image pixels, converted to grey size, and centered to a fixed size. This is a small dataset on which an algorithm can be quickly tested. In the next section, we will see how to load this dataset to be used in TensorFlow.

Loading the MNIST data

Load the `MNIST` data directly from TensorFlow. Note that we specify one hot encoding as an argument while loading the data. The label is stored as integers but should be loaded as one-hot encoding in-order to train. It is assumed that the reader is running the code from an editor with TensorFlow imported `tf` from this point onward. The following is the code snippet to load `MNIST_data`:

```
from tensorflow.examples.tutorials.mnist import input_data
mnist_data = input_data.read_data_sets('MNIST_data', one_hot=True)
```

For the first run, the data will be downloaded and may take some time. From the second run, the cached data will be utilized. In the next section, we will build a perceptron to classify the digits.

Building a perceptron

A perceptron is a single-layer neural network. The concepts covered in this chapter, such as a fully connected layer, `activation` function, Stochastic Gradient Descent, `logits`, one hot encoding, softmax, and cross-entropy will be useful here. You will learn how to define these components of neural networks in TensorFlow and use the network to train the `MNIST` data.

Defining placeholders for input data and targets

A placeholder is a tensor where the data is passed. Placeholders aren't specific values but will receive input during computation. The input size of the perceptron, number of classes, batch size, and the total number of iterations or batches are first declared. `x_input` is the input where the images will be fed later. `y_input` is the placeholder where the one-shot labels or targets will be supplied as shown here:

```
input_size = 784
no_classes = 10
batch_size = 100
total_batches = 200

x_input = tf.placeholder(tf.float32, shape=[None, input_size])
y_input = tf.placeholder(tf.float32, shape=[None, no_classes])
```

The None in the shape argument indicates that it can be of any size as we have not yet defined the batch size. The second argument is the size of the tensor for x_input and the number of classes for y_input. Based on the type of placeholder, we have sent the data as floats. Next, we can define the perceptron.

Defining the variables for a fully connected layer

Let's define a simple linear classifier or perceptron by explaining the variables such as weights and bias. The values of these variables will be learned during computation. These are also referred to as parameters of the model. The weight variables are initialized with normal random distribution with the shape of input size and number of classes. The input size is 784 here as the image is reshaped into a single vector. The number of classes is 10 which is equal to the number of digits in the dataset. The bias variable is also initialized with random normal distribution with the size equal to the number of classes. The weights and bias are defined as follows:

```
weights = tf.Variable(tf.random_normal([input_size, no_classes]))
bias = tf.Variable(tf.random_normal([no_classes]))
```

The initialization of the variables can be zeroes but a random normal distribution gives a steady training. The inputs are then weighted and added with the bias to produce logits as shown next:

```
logits = tf.matmul(x_input, weights) + bias
```

The logits produced by the perceptron has to be compared against one-hot labels y_input. As learned in Chapter 1, *Getting Started*, it is better to use softmax coupled with cross-entropy for comparing logits and one-hot labels.

The tf.nn.softmax_cross_entropy_with_logits API from TensorFlow does this for us. The loss can be computed by averaging the cross-entropies. Then the cross-entropy is fed through gradient descent optimization done by tf.train.GradientDescentOptimizer. The optimizer takes the loss and minimizes it with a learning rate of 0.5. The computation of softmax, cross-entropy, loss, optimization is shown next:

```
softmax_cross_entropy = tf.nn.softmax_cross_entropy_with_logits(
    labels=y_input, logits=logits)
loss_operation = tf.reduce_mean(softmax_cross_entropy)
optimiser = tf.train.GradientDescentOptimizer(
    learning_rate=0.5).minimize(loss_operation)
```

The softmax and cross-entropies are computed together from the `tf.nn` package, which has several other useful methods. The `tf.train` has several optimizers, and here, we are using the vanilla gradient descent. You can visit TensorFlow API documentation to understand other optional parameters. Until now, the placeholders, variables, and operations are defined and yet to be populated with tensors.

> Read the list of optimizers available in TensorFlow at `https://www.tensorflow.org/api_guides/python/train`. The Adam optimizer is particularly useful for computer vision applications. It generally converges faster and we need not define a learning rate to start with. For a theoretical summary of optimizers, visit `http://ruder.io/optimizing-gradient-descent`.

Training the model with data

Now you have defined the model and training operation. The next step is to start training the model with the data. During training, the gradients are calculated and the weights are updated. The variables have not yet been initialized. Next, start the session and initialize the variables using a global variable initializer:

```
session = tf.Session()
session.run(tf.global_variables_initializer())
```

The preceding two lines are required for most of the examples in this book. It is assumed that the reader will use these two lines wherever required. Now the graph is ready to be fed with data and start training. Over a loop, read the data in batches and train the model. Training the model is carried out by running the session with the required tensors. The optimizer has to be called in order for the graph to update the weights:

```
for batch_no in range(total_batches):
    mnist_batch = mnist_data.train.next_batch(batch_size)
    _, loss_value = session.run([optimiser, loss_operation], feed_dict={
        x_input: mnist_batch[0],
        y_input: mnist_batch[1]
    })
    print(loss_value)
```

The first argument of the `run` method can have an array for which the outputs of the values are requested. We pass loss because printing loss tells us whether the model is getting trained or not. The loss is expected to decrease as we are minimizing the loss. The feed dict is a Python dictionary used to directly feed the input and target labels to the placeholders. Once this loop ends, the loss should be generally lower than 0.46. Next, we can evaluate how well the model worked by computing the accuracy, as shown here:

```
predictions = tf.argmax(logits, 1)
correct_predictions = tf.equal(predictions, tf.argmax(y_input, 1))
accuracy_operation = tf.reduce_mean(tf.cast(correct_predictions,
                                    tf.float32))
test_images, test_labels = mnist_data.test.images, mnist_data.test.labels
accuracy_value = session.run(accuracy_operation, feed_dict={
    x_input: test_images,
    y_input: test_labels
})
print('Accuracy : ', accuracy_value)
session.close()
```

The prediction should be the index of the maximum activation. It should be compared with the ground truth on MNIST labels for correct predictions. The accuracy is calculated using the average of correct predictions. The accuracy of the data can be evaluated by running the session with test data as the feed dictionary. When the whole program is run, it should finally produce an accuracy of around **90%**. The definition of the model may seem too explicit without simpler APIs for training and testing. This level of basic definition gives the power of expressiveness for TensorFlow. In the next sections, we will see higher level APIs. The accuracy obtained by the perceptron is not great, and in the next section, we will use a deeper network with convolution layers to improve the accuracy.

Building a multilayer convolutional network

In this section, we will see how to create a multilayer convolutional network in TensorFlow and watch how a deeper network improves classification accuracy. We will define the layers with TensorFlow layers' APIs rather than defining them from scratch. The best practice methods are engrained in those methods. The import of libraries, datasets, and placeholders can be followed from the previous section. This time, we will use TensorBoard for visualizing the training process. In order to visualize the statistics of the variables, the values of variable statistics have to be added to `tf.summary`.

The summaries will be written to a folder that is interpretable to TensorBoard. Let's define a function to write the summaries so that TensorBoard can be used to visualize them:

```
def add_variable_summary(tf_variable, summary_name):
  with tf.name_scope(summary_name + '_summary'):
    mean = tf.reduce_mean(tf_variable)
    tf.summary.scalar('Mean', mean)
    with tf.name_scope('standard_deviation'):
        standard_deviation = tf.sqrt(tf.reduce_mean(
            tf.square(tf_variable - mean)))
    tf.summary.scalar('StandardDeviation', standard_deviation)
    tf.summary.scalar('Maximum', tf.reduce_max(tf_variable))
    tf.summary.scalar('Minimum', tf.reduce_min(tf_variable))
    tf.summary.histogram('Histogram', tf_variable)
```

The variable `summary` function writes the summaries of a variable. There are five statistics added to the summaries: mean, standard deviation, maximum, minimum and histogram. Summaries can be either a `scalar` or a `histogram`. We will see how these values can be visualized in TensorBoard when logged for several variables. Unlike the previous model, we will resize the `MNIST` data into a square and use it like a two-dimensional image. The following is the command to reshape the image into 28 image pixels by 28 image pixels:

```
x_input_reshape = tf.reshape(x_input, [-1, 28, 28, 1],
    name='input_reshape')
```

The dimension -1 denotes that the batch size can be any number. Note that there is an argument called `name` that will be reflected in the TensorBoard graph for ease of understanding. We will define a 2D convolution layer where the input, filters, kernels, and activations are defined. This method can be called anywhere for further examples and is useful when the activation function has to have **Rectified Linear Unit (ReLU)** activation. The `convolution` function layer is defined as follows:

```
def convolution_layer(input_layer, filters, kernel_size=[3, 3],
                    activation=tf.nn.relu):
    layer = tf.layers.conv2d(
        inputs=input_layer,
        filters=filters,
        kernel_size=kernel_size,
        activation=activation,
    )
    add_variable_summary(layer, 'convolution')
    return layer
```

There are default parameters for `kernel_size` and `activation`. The summaries are added to the layer within the function and the layer is returned. Whenever the function is called, `input_layer` has to be passed as a parameter. This definition will make our other code simple and small. In a very similar way, we will define a function for the `pooling_layer` as follows:

```
def pooling_layer(input_layer, pool_size=[2, 2], strides=2):
    layer = tf.layers.max_pooling2d(
        inputs=input_layer,
        pool_size=pool_size,
        strides=strides
    )
    add_variable_summary(layer, 'pooling')
    return layer
```

This layer has default parameters for `pool_size` and `strides` to be `[2, 2]` and 2 respectively. These parameters generally work well but can be changed when necessary. The summaries are added for this layer too. We will next define a dense layer as follows:

```
def dense_layer(input_layer, units, activation=tf.nn.relu):
    layer = tf.layers.dense(
        inputs=input_layer,
        units=units,
        activation=activation
    )
    add_variable_summary(layer, 'dense')
    return layer
```

The dense layer defined has default parameters for activation and variable summaries are added as well. The `pooling_layer` takes the feature map from the convolution layer and reduces it to half its size by skipping, using the pool size and strides. All these layers are connected as a graph and are just defined. None of the values is initialized. Another convolution layer can be added to transform the sampled features from the first convolution layer to better features. After pooling, we may reshape the activations to a linear fashion in order to be fed through dense layers:

```
convolution_layer_1 = convolution_layer(x_input_reshape, 64)
pooling_layer_1 = pooling_layer(convolution_layer_1)
convolution_layer_2 = convolution_layer(pooling_layer_1, 128)
pooling_layer_2 = pooling_layer(convolution_layer_2)
flattened_pool = tf.reshape(pooling_layer_2, [-1, 5 * 5 * 128],
                            name='flattened_pool')
dense_layer_bottleneck = dense_layer(flattened_pool, 1024)
```

The only difference between the convolution layers is the filter size. It's important that the dimensions change appropriately from layer to layer. Choosing the parameters for kernel and stride are arbitrary and these numbers are chosen by experience. Two convolution layers are defined, and this can be followed by a fully connected layer. A dense-layer API can take any vector of a single dimension and map it to any number of hidden units, as in this case is `1024`. The hidden layer is followed by ReLU activation to make this a non-linear computation. Variable summaries are added for this layer as well. This is followed by a dropout layer with a rate of dropping out. Keeping this high will stop the network from learning. The training mode can be set to `True` and `False` based on when we use this. We will set this as `True` (default is `False`) for the training. We will have to change this while the accuracy is calculated. Hence, a bool is kept for this, that will be fed during training:

```
dropout_bool = tf.placeholder(tf.bool)
dropout_layer = tf.layers.dropout(
        inputs=dense_layer_bottleneck,
        rate=0.4,
        training=dropout_bool
    )
```

The dropout layer is fed again to a dense layer, which is called logits. Logits is the final layer with activations leading to the number of classes. The activations will be spiked for a particular class, which is the target class, and can be obtained for a maximum of those 10 activations:

```
logits = dense_layer(dropout_layer, no_classes)
```

The logits output is very similar to the model created in the previous section. Now the logits can be passed through the softmax layer followed by the cross-entropy calculation as before. Here, we have added a scope name to get a better visualization in TensorBoard as follows:

```
with tf.name_scope('loss'):
    softmax_cross_entropy = tf.nn.softmax_cross_entropy_with_logits(
        labels=y_input, logits=logits)
    loss_operation = tf.reduce_mean(softmax_cross_entropy, name='loss')
    tf.summary.scalar('loss', loss_operation)
```

This `loss` function can be optimized with `tf.train` APIs' methods. Here, we will use the `Adamoptimiser`. The learning rate need not be defined and works well for most cases:

```
with tf.name_scope('optimiser'):
    optimiser = tf.train.AdamOptimizer().minimize(loss_operation)
```

The accuracy is calculated as before but name scopes are added for correct predictions and accuracy calculation:

```
with tf.name_scope('accuracy'):
    with tf.name_scope('correct_prediction'):
        predictions = tf.argmax(logits, 1)
        correct_predictions = tf.equal(predictions, tf.argmax(y_input, 1))
    with tf.name_scope('accuracy'):
        accuracy_operation = tf.reduce_mean(
            tf.cast(correct_predictions, tf.float32))
tf.summary.scalar('accuracy', accuracy_operation)
```

A scalar summary for accuracy is also added. The next step is to start the session and initialize the variables as in the previous section. The lines are not repeated here. The summaries have to be merged, and the files for writing the training and testing summaries have to be defined:

```
merged_summary_operation = tf.summary.merge_all()
train_summary_writer = tf.summary.FileWriter('/tmp/train', session.graph)
test_summary_writer = tf.summary.FileWriter('/tmp/test')
```

Note that the graph is written once with the `summary_writer`. The training is very similar to before except that the accuracy calculations while training and the values are added to the summaries. Next, the data can be loaded in batches and training can be started:

```
test_images, test_labels = mnist_data.test.images, mnist_data.test.labels

for batch_no in range(total_batches):
    mnist_batch = mnist_data.train.next_batch(batch_size)
    train_images, train_labels = mnist_batch[0], mnist_batch[1]
    _, merged_summary = session.run([optimiser, merged_summary_operation],
                                    feed_dict={
        x_input: train_images,
        y_input: train_labels,
        dropout_bool: True
    })
    train_summary_writer.add_summary(merged_summary, batch_no)
    if batch_no % 10 == 0:
        merged_summary, _ = session.run([merged_summary_operation,
                                        accuracy_operation], feed_dict={
            x_input: test_images,
            y_input: test_labels,
            dropout_bool: False
        })
        test_summary_writer.add_summary(merged_summary, batch_no)
```

Summaries are returned in every iteration for training data and are added to the writer. For every tenth iteration, the test summaries are added. Note that the dropout is enabled only during training and not during testing. We have completed the definition, and summaries of the network and this can be run. To see the training process, we can go to TensorBoard as described in `Chapter 1`, *Getting Started*.

Utilizing TensorBoard in deep learning

Once the TensorBoard is opened in the browser, go to the **Graphs** tab. The graph that we have defined and been getting trained should be displayed. Right-clicking on the nodes, we can choose the operations to be removed from the main graph. After some alignment, the graph should look as follows:

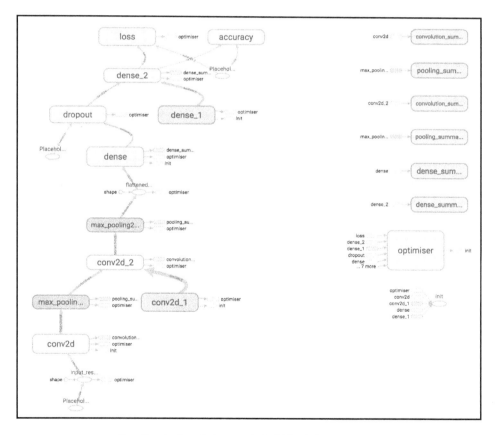

Figure illustrating the graphs that were trained and defined in the previous instance

Notice how nicely all the layers that we have defined are displayed. This is very useful to check the definition of the architecture. The direction of the graph is nicely visualized with all the particulars. By clicking on each node, you can see the particulars of the node, such as input and output tensor shapes, as shown here:

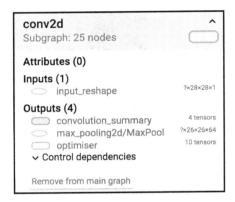

These values can be used to cross-check the definitions of the parameters of the layers. Make yourself familiar with this page by noticing the legend in the bottom left, as follows:

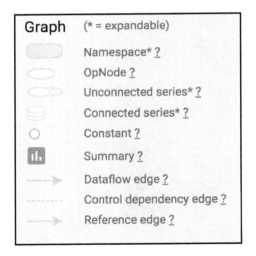

The name scopes are grouped and individual components can be seen by clicking on the plus sign on the nodes. The nodes are arranged by colors. Now we can move to the scalars page. By moving around the page, you can spot the accuracy graphs, as shown in the following figure:

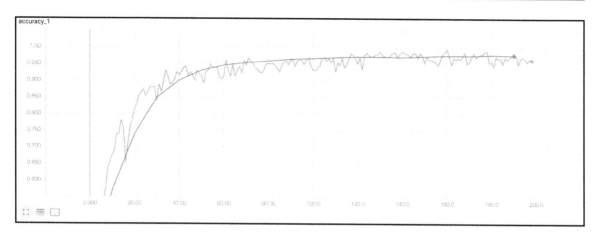

The orange line is for training data and the blue line for testing data. They roughly follow the same pattern. There are slightly lesser bright lines indicating the original values, whereas the brighter ones are smoothed curves. The smoothing coefficient can be selected in the UI. The accuracy of the test data has reached above 97%. The following is the figure from the loss summary:

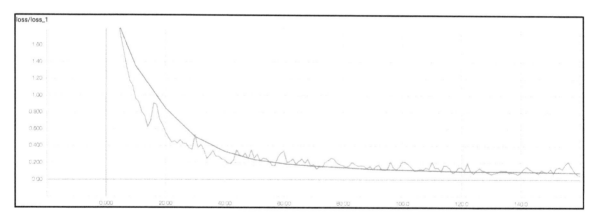

The loss was steadily decreasing for both training and testing data during the training process, which is a good sign. The data of all the summaries will be refreshed during the training process, and we can witness the increase in accuracy with a decrease in the loss to achieve an excellent result of 97.38% test accuracy.

This helps you see whether the model is learning and moving toward better results. The other summaries such as min, max, mean, and standard deviation are also useful. The following are the graphs of a dense layer:

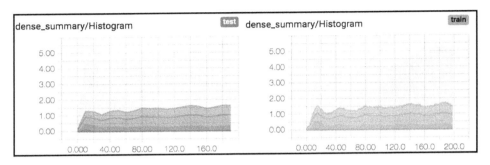

These summaries are useful to notice the change in weights. These distributions can also be visualized as histograms, as follows:

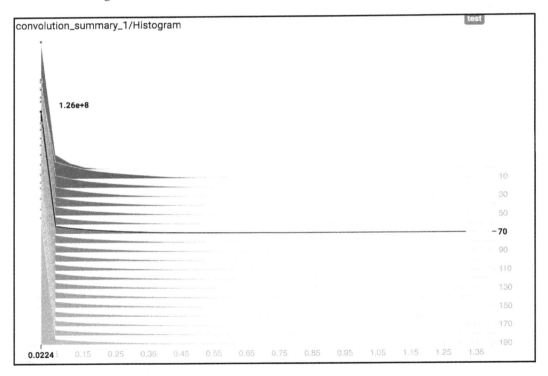

These are the spreads of the weights of the logits. These are the beautiful visualizations possible with TensorBoard and are extremely helpful in training. By making the model deeper, we were able to witness a huge increase in accuracy. In the next section, we will see how to train the same model with Keras APIs. Now you can see the power of TensorBoard in inspecting the deep learning model and the training process.

Training the MNIST model in Keras

In this section, we will use the same model as defined in the previous section using `tf.keras` APIs. It is better to learn both Keras and layers packages from TensorFlow as they could be seen at several open source codes. The objective of the book is to make you understand various offerings of TensorFlow so that you can build products on top of it.

"Code is read more often than it is written."

Bearing in mind the preceding quote, you are shown how to implement the same model using various APIs. Open source code of any implementation of the latest algorithms will be a mix of these APIs. Next, we will start with the Keras implementation.

Preparing the dataset

The `MNIST` data is available with Keras. First, import `tensorflow`. Then define a few constants such as batch size, the classes, and the number of epochs. The batch size can be selected based on the RAM available on your machine. The higher the batch size, the more RAM required. The impact of the batch size on the accuracy is minimal. The number of classes is equal to 10 here and will be different for different problems. The number of epochs determines how many times the training has to go through the full dataset. If the loss is reduced at the end of all epochs, it can be set to a high number. In a few cases, training longer could give better accuracy. Let us now look at the steps to create the dataset:

1. Set the dimensions of the input images as well as follows:

```
batch_size = 128
no_classes = 10
epochs = 2
image_height, image_width = 28, 28
```

2. Load the data from disk to memory using the Keras utilities:

```
(x_train, y_train), (x_test, y_test) =
tf.keras.datasets.mnist.load_data()
```

3. Reshape the vector into an image format, and define the input dimension for the convolution using the code given:

```
x_train = x_train.reshape(x_train.shape[0], image_height,
image_width, 1)
x_test = x_test.reshape(x_test.shape[0], image_height, image_width,
1)
input_shape = (image_height, image_width, 1)
```

4. Convert the data type to `float` as follows:

```
x_train = x_train.astype('float32')
x_test = x_test.astype('float32')
```

5. Normalize the data by subtracting the mean of the data:

```
x_train /= 255
x_test /= 255
```

6. Convert the categorical labels to one-shot encoding:

```
y_train = tf.keras.utils.to_categorical(y_train, no_classes)
y_test = tf.keras.utils.to_categorical(y_test, no_classes)
```

This is very different from the TensorFlow way of writing the code. The data is loaded already in memory and none of the concepts of `Placeholders` is present here.

Building the model

In this section, we will use a few convolution layers followed by fully connected layers for training the preceding dataset. Construct a simple sequential model with two convolution layers followed by pooling, dropout, and dense layers. A sequential model has the add method to stack layers one above another. The first layer has 64 filters, and the second layers have 128 filters. The kernel size is 3 for all the filters. Apply the max pooling after the convolution layers. The output of the convolution layers is flattened connecting to a couple of fully connected layers with dropout connections.

The last layer is connected to softmax as this is a multiclass classification problem. The following code shows how to define the model:

```
def simple_cnn(input_shape):
    model = tf.keras.models.Sequential()
    model.add(tf.keras.layers.Conv2D(
        filters=64,
        kernel_size=(3, 3),
        activation='relu',
        input_shape=input_shape
    ))
    model.add(tf.keras.layers.Conv2D(
        filters=128,
        kernel_size=(3, 3),
        activation='relu'
    ))
    model.add(tf.keras.layers.MaxPooling2D(pool_size=(2, 2)))
    model.add(tf.keras.layers.Dropout(rate=0.3))
    model.add(tf.keras.layers.Flatten())
    model.add(tf.keras.layers.Dense(units=1024, activation='relu'))
    model.add(tf.keras.layers.Dropout(rate=0.3))
    model.add(tf.keras.layers.Dense(units=no_classes,
activation='softmax'))
    model.compile(loss=tf.keras.losses.categorical_crossentropy,
                  optimizer=tf.keras.optimizers.Adam(),
                  metrics=['accuracy'])
    return model
simple_cnn_model = simple_cnn(input_shape)
```

The model is just defined and has to be compiled. During compilation loss, optimizer and metrics have to be defined. The loss will be cross-entropy, optimized by the Adam algorithm, and we will report the accuracy as the metric. Using the loaded data, train and evaluate the data. Load the training data with the training parameters and fit the model:

```
simple_cnn_model.fit(x_train, y_train, batch_size, epochs, (x_test,
y_test))
train_loss, train_accuracy = simple_cnn_model.evaluate(
    x_train, y_train, verbose=0)
print('Train data loss:', train_loss)
print('Train data accuracy:', train_accuracy)
```

A session is not created when Keras APIs are used. Then evaluate the test data as follows:

```
test_loss, test_accuracy = simple_cnn_model.evaluate(
    x_test, y_test, verbose=0)
print('Test data loss:', test_loss)
print('Test data accuracy:', test_accuracy)
```

The evaluation is also created without any explicit creation of the session. After finishing the run, the result should look similar to the following:

```
Loss for train data: 0.0171295607952
Accuracy of train data: 0.995016666667
Loss for test data: 0.0282736890309
Accuracy of test data: 0.9902
```

This should give a better accuracy of 99% on the test data. Note that the training accuracy is higher than the test data, and it's always a good practice to print both of them. The difference in accuracy is due to the number of iterations. The accuracy is a bit more than the previous model created in TensorFlow because of the difference in the dataset.

Other popular image testing datasets

The MNIST dataset is the most commonly used dataset for testing the algorithms. But there are other datasets that are used to test image classification algorithms.

The CIFAR dataset

The **Canadian Institute for Advanced Research (CIFAR)**-10 dataset has 60,000 images with 50,000 images for training and 10,000 images for testing. The number of classes is 10. The image dimension is 32 pixels by 32 pixels. The following are randomly selected images from each of the class:

The images are tiny and just contain one object. The CIFAR-100 dataset contains the same number of images but with 100 classes. Hence, there are only 600 images per class. Each image comes with a super label and a fine label. This dataset is available at tf.keras.datasets if you wish to experiment.

The Fashion-MNIST dataset

Fashion-MNIST is a dataset created as an alternative to the MNIST dataset. This dataset created as MNIST is considered as too easy and this can be directly replaced with MNIST.

The following is randomly selected examples from the dataset after **principal component analysis (PCA)** is performed:

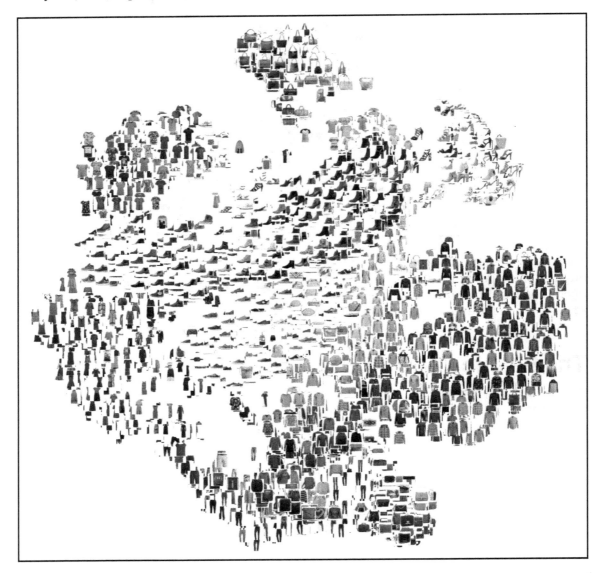

The dataset size, number of labels and image size are similar to MNIST. More details can be found at https://github.com/zalandoresearch/fashion-mnist. You can run the models learned previously and check the accuracy.

The ImageNet dataset and competition

ImageNet is a computer vision dataset with 14,197,122 images, 21,841 Synsets indexed. Synset is a node in WordNet hierarchy that in turn is a set of synonyms. There is a competition held every year with 1,000 classes from this dataset. It has been the standard benchmark for assessing the performance of image classification algorithms.

In 2013, a deep learning based computer vision model got the number one spot. From then, only deep learning models have won the competition. The following is the top five error rate over the years in the competition:

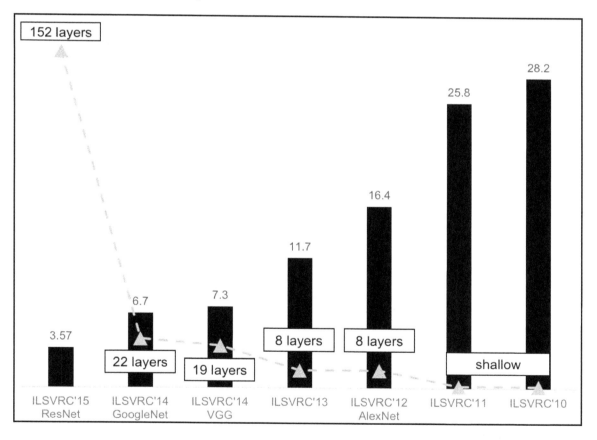

You can notice that the accuracy has been increasing over the years, as well as the depth of the layers. Next, we will understand the models that are present in this graph.

The bigger deep learning models

We will go through several model definitions that have achieved state-of-the-art results in the ImageNet competitions. We will look at them individually on the following topics.

The AlexNet model

AlexNet is the first publication that started a wide interest in deep learning for computer vision. Krizhevsky et al. (`https://papers.nips.cc/paper/4824-imagenet-classification-with-deep-convolutional-neural-networks.pdf`) proposed AlexNet and it has been a pioneer and influential in this field. This model won the ImageNet 2013 challenge. The error rate was 15.4%, which was significantly better than the next. The model was relatively a simple architecture with five convolution layers. The challenge was to classify 1,000 categories of objects. The image and data had 15 million annotated images with over 22,000 categories. Out of them, only a 1,000 categories are used for the competition. AlexNet used ReLU as the activation function and found it was training several times faster than other activation functions. The architecture of the model is shown here:

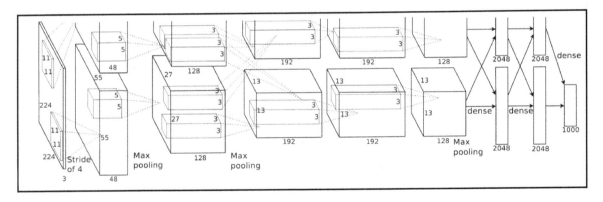

Reproduced with permission from Krizhevsky et al.

The paper also used data augmentation techniques such as image translations, horizontal flips, and random cropping. The dropout layer prevents overfitting. The model used vanilla **Stochastic Gradient Descent** (**SGD**) for training. The parameters of SGD are chosen carefully for training. The learning rate changes over a fixed set of training iterations. The momentum and weight decay take fixed values for training. There is a concept called **Local Response Normalization** (**LRN**) introduced in this paper. The LRN layers normalize every pixel across the filters to avoid huge activation in a particular filter.

This layer is not used anymore as recent research suggests that there is not much improvement because of LRN. AlexNet has 60 million parameters in total.

The VGG-16 model

The **VGG** model stands for the **Visual Geometry Group** from Oxford. The model was very simple and had a greater depth than AlexNet. The paper had two models with 16 and 19 layers depth. All the CNN layers were using 3 by 3 filters with stride and a pad of size 1 and a max pooling size of 2 with stride 2. This resulted in a decrease in the number of parameters. Though the size is decreasing because of max pooling, the number of filters is increasing with layers. The architecture of the 16-layer deep model is as follows:

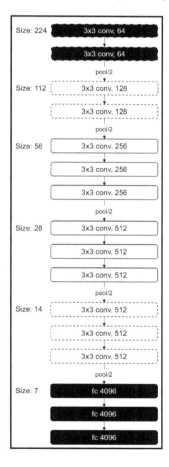

This model has 138 million parameters and is the largest of all the models described here. But the uniformity of parameters is quite good. The characteristic is such that, as deep as the network gets, the smaller the image is with an increased number of filters. One of the data augmentation techniques used was scale jittering. Scale jittering is an augmentation technique where a side with random size is considered to vary the scales.

The Google Inception-V3 model

Inception-V3 was proposed by Szegedy et al. (`https://arxiv.org/pdf/1409.4842.pdf`) and introduced the concept of inception that has a better way of generalization. This was the architecture that won the ImageNet competition in 2014. It is geared towards efficiency for speed and size. It has 12 times lesser parameters than AlexNet. Inception is the micro-architecture on which a macro-architecture is built. Each hidden layer has a higher-level representation of the image. At each layer, we have an option of using pooling or other layers. Instead of using one type of kernel, inception uses several kernels. An average pooling is followed by various size convolutions and then they are concatenated.

The kernel parameters can be learned based on the data. Using several kernels, the model can detect small features as well as higher abstractions. The 1 x 1 convolution will reduce the feature and, hence, computations. This takes less RAM during inference. The following is the inception module in its simplest form where there are options of convolutions with various kernel sizes and pooling:

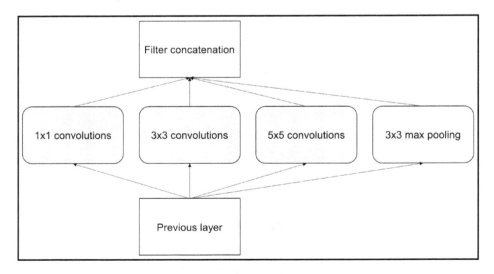

Notice that operations are happening in parallel, as opposed to AlexNet or VGG. The output volume is huge, and hence, 1 x 1 filters are introduced for dimensionality reduction. When the reduced dimensions are added to the architecture it becomes as follows:

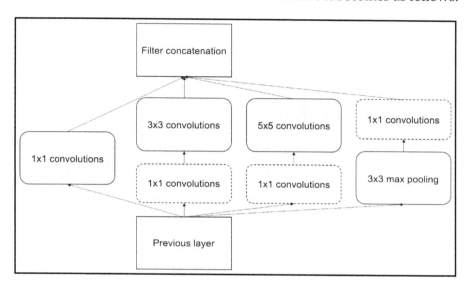

The whole architecture of the model is as follows with all the bells and whistles:

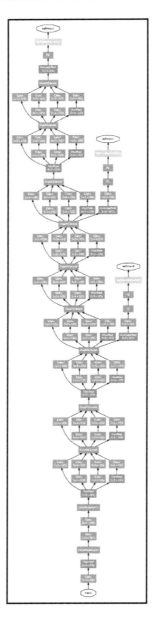

Figure illustrating the Google Inception V3 model architecture [Reproduced with permission from Szegedy et al.]

There are nine inception modules with a total of 100 layers and they achieve good performance.

The Microsoft ResNet-50 model

ResNet was proposed by He et al. (`https://arxiv.org/pdf/1512.03385.pdf`) and won the ImageNet competition in 2015. This method showed that deeper networks can be trained. The deeper the network, the more saturated the accuracy becomes. It's not even due to overfitting or due to the presence of a high number of parameters, but due to a reduction in the training error. This is due to the inability to backpropagate the gradients. This can be overcome by sending the gradients directly to the deeper layers with a residual block as follows:

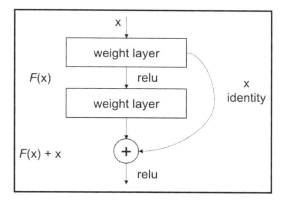

Every two layers are connected forming a residual block. You can see that the training is passed between the layers. By this technique, the backpropagation can carry the error to earlier layers.

 The model definitions can be used from `https://github.com/ tensorflow/tensorflow/tree/r1.4/tensorflow/python/keras/_impl/ keras/applications`. Every layer in the model is defined and pre-trained weights on the `ImageNet` dataset are available.

The SqueezeNet model

The **SqueezeNet** model was introduced by Iandola et al. (`https://arxiv.org/pdf/1602. 07360.pdf`), to reduce the model size and the number of parameters.

The network was made smaller by replacing 3 x 3 filters with 1 x 1 filters as shown here:

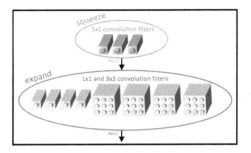

Reproduced with permission from Iandola et al.

The number of inputs of the 3 x 3 filters has also reduced downsampling of the layers when happening at the higher level, providing large activation maps:

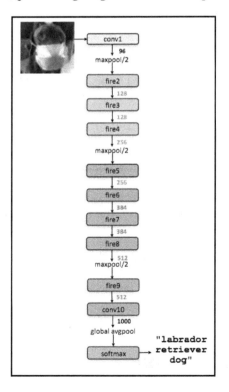

Reproduced with permission from Iandola et al.

Spatial transformer networks

The **spatial transformer networks** proposed by Jaderberg et al. (`https://arxiv.org/pdf/1506.02025.pdf`) try to transform the image before passing to the CNN. This is different from other networks because it tries to modify the image before convolution. This network learns the parameters to transform the image. The parameters are learned for an **affine transformation**. By applying an affine transformation, **spatial invariance** is achieved. In the previous networks, spatial invariance was achieved by max-pooling layers. The placement of spatial transformer networks is shown as follows:

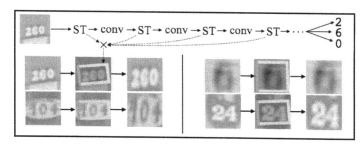

Reproduced with permission from Jaderberg et al.

The DenseNet model

DenseNet is an extension of ResNet proposed by Huang et al. (`https://arxiv.org/pdf/1608.06993.pdf`). In ResNet blocks, the previous layer is merged into the future layer by summation. In DenseNet, the previous layer is merged into the future layer by concatenation. DenseNet connects all the layers to the previous layers and the current layer to the following layers.

In the following diagram, it can be seen how the feature maps are supplied as input to the other layers:

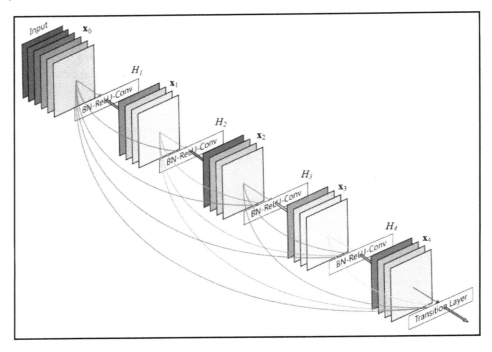

Reproduced with permission from Huang et al.

This way, it provides several advantages such as smoother gradients, feature transformation and so on. This also reduces the number of parameters:

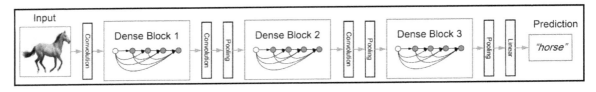

Reproduced with permission from Huang et al.

We have covered all the latest algorithms for the image classification task. Any of the architectures can be used for an image classification task. In the next section, we will see how to train a model to predict pets, using these advanced architectures and improve the accuracy.

Training a model for cats versus dogs

In this section, we will prepare and train a model for predicting cats versus dogs and understand some techniques which increase the accuracy. Most of the image classification problems come into this paradigm. Techniques covered in this section, such as augmentation and transfer learning, are useful for several problems.

Preparing the data

For the purpose of classification, we will download the data from **kaggle** and store in an appropriate format. Sign up and log in to www.kaggle.com and go to https://www.kaggle.com/c/dogs-vs-cats/data. Download the train.zip and test1.zip files from that page. The train.zip file contains 25,000 images of pet data. We will use only a portion of the data to train a model. Readers with more computing power, such as a **Graphics Processing Unit (GPU)**, can use more data than suggested. Run the following script to rearrange the images and create the necessary folders:

```
import os
import shutil

work_dir = '' # give your correct directory
image_names = sorted(os.listdir(os.path.join(work_dir, 'train')))


def copy_files(prefix_str, range_start, range_end, target_dir):
    image_paths = [os.path.join(work_dir, 'train', prefix_str + '.' +
str(i) + '.jpg')
                   for i in range(range_start, range_end)]
    dest_dir = os.path.join(work_dir, 'data', target_dir, prefix_str)
    os.makedirs(dest_dir)
    for image_path in image_paths:
        shutil.copy(image_path, dest_dir)


copy_files('dog', 0, 1000, 'train')
copy_files('cat', 0, 1000, 'train')
copy_files('dog', 1000, 1400, 'test')
copy_files('cat', 1000, 1400, 'test')
```

For our experiments, we will use only 1,000 images of cats and dogs. So, copy images 0–999 from the downloaded folder to the newly created `train` folder under `cats`. Similarly, copy 1,000–1,400 to `data/test/cat`, 10–999 in `train/dogs` and 1,000–1,400 in `data/test/dog` so that we have 1,000 training examples for each class and 400 validation examples for each class.

Benchmarking with simple CNN

Let's run the previous `simple_cnn` model on this dataset and see how it performs. This model's performance will be the basic benchmark against which we judge other techniques. We will define a few variables for data loading and training, as shown here:

```
image_height, image_width = 150, 150
train_dir = os.path.join(work_dir, 'train')
test_dir = os.path.join(work_dir, 'test')
no_classes = 2
no_validation = 800
epochs = 2
batch_size = 200
no_train = 2000
no_test = 800
input_shape = (image_height, image_width, 3)
epoch_steps = no_train // batch_size
test_steps = no_test // batch_size
```

This constant is used for the techniques discussed in this section of training a model for predicting cats and dogs. Here, we are using 2,800 images to train and test which is reasonable for a personal computer's RAM. But this is not sustainable for bigger datasets. It's better if we load only a batch of images at a time for training and testing. For this purpose, a `tf.keras` has a class called `ImageDataGenerator` that reads images whenever necessary. It is assumed that a `simple_cnn` model is imported from the previous section. The following is an example of using a generator for loading the images:

```
generator_train =
tf.keras.preprocessing.image.ImageDataGenerator(rescale=1. / 255)
generator_test = tf.keras.preprocessing.image.ImageDataGenerator(rescale=1.
/ 255)
```

This definition also rescales the images when it is loaded. Next, we can read the images from the directory using the `flow_from_directory` method as follows:

```
train_images = generator_train.flow_from_directory(
    train_dir,
    batch_size=batch_size,
    target_size=(image_width, image_height))

test_images = generator_test.flow_from_directory(
    test_dir,
    batch_size=batch_size,
    target_size=(image_width, image_height))
```

The directory to load the images, size of batches and target size for the images are passed as an argument. This method performs the rescaling and passes the data in batches for fitting the model. This generator can be directly used for fitting the model. The method `fit_generator` of the model can be used as follows:

```
simple_cnn_model.fit_generator(
    train_images,
    steps_per_epoch=epoch_steps,
    epochs=epochs,
    validation_data=test_images,
    validation_steps=test_steps)
```

This model fits the data from the generator of training images. The number of epochs is defined from training, and validation data is passed for getting the performance of the model overtraining. This `fit_generator` enables parallel processing of data and model training. The CPU performs the rescaling while the GPU can perform the model training. This gives the high efficiency of computing resources. After 50 epochs, this model should give an accuracy of 60%. Next, we will see how to augment the dataset to get an improved performance.

Augmenting the dataset

Data augmentation gives ways to increase the size of the dataset. Data augmentation introduces noise during training, producing robustness in the model to various inputs. This technique is useful in scenarios when the dataset is small and can be combined and used with other techniques. Next, we will see the different types of augmentation.

Augmentation techniques

There are various ways to augment the images as described as follows:

- **Flipping**: The image is mirrored or flipped in a horizontal or vertical direction
- **Random Cropping**: Random portions are cropped, hence the model can deal with occlusions
- **Shearing**: The images are deformed to affect the shape of the objects
- **Zooming**: Zoomed portions of images are trained to deal with varying scales of images
- **Rotation**: The objects are rotated to deal with various degrees of change in objects
- **Whitening**: The whitening is done by a Principal Component Analysis that preserves only the important data
- **Normalization**: Normalizes the pixels by standardizing the mean and variance
- **Channel shifting**: The color channels are shifted to make the model robust to color changes caused by various artifacts

All these techniques are implemented in `ImageDataGenerator` to increase the dataset size. The following is a modified version of `generator_train` with some augmentation techniques discussed previously:

```
generator_train = tf.keras.preprocessing.image.ImageDataGenerator(
    rescale=1. / 255,
    horizontal_flip=True,
    zoom_range=0.3,
    shear_range=0.3,)
```

Replacing the `generator_train` in the preceding code will increase the accuracy to 90%. Change the parameters of augmentation and notice the changes. We will discuss a technique called transfer learning in the following section, which helps in training bigger models with fewer data.

Transfer learning or fine-tuning of a model

Transfer learning is the process of learning from a pre-trained model that was trained on a larger dataset. Training a model with random initialization often takes time and energy to get the result. Initializing the model with a pre-trained model gives faster convergence, saving time and energy. These models that are pre-trained are often trained with carefully chosen hyperparameters.

Either the several layers of the pre-trained model can be used without any modification, or can be bit trained to adapt to the changes. In this section, we will learn how to fine-tune or transfer learning for a model that was trained on the `ImageNet` dataset with millions of classes.

Training on bottleneck features

The models that are covered in the previous sections are simple and hence, may yield less accuracy. Complex models should be built from them. They cannot be built from scratch. Hence, bottleneck features are extracted and the classifier is trained on them. Bottleneck features are the features that are produced by complex architectures training several million images. The images are done with a forward pass and the pre-final layer features are stored. From these, a simple logistic classifier is trained for classification. Extract the bottleneck layers as follows:

```
generator = tf.keras.preprocessing.image.ImageDataGenerator(rescale=1. /
255)

model = tf.keras.applications.VGG16(include_top=False)

train_images = generator.flow_from_directory(
    train_dir,
    batch_size=batch_size,
    target_size=(image_width, image_height),
    class_mode=None,
    shuffle=False
)
train_bottleneck_features = model.predict_generator(train_images,
epoch_steps)

test_images = generator.flow_from_directory(
    test_dir,
    batch_size=batch_size,
    target_size=(image_width, image_height),
    class_mode=None,
    shuffle=False
)

test_bottleneck_features = model.predict_generator(test_images, test_steps)
```

The VGG model is taken and used to predict the images. The labels are assigned as follows:

```
train_labels = np.array([0] * int(no_train / 2) + [1] * int(no_train / 2))
test_labels = np.array([0] * int(no_test / 2) + [1] * int(no_test / 2))
```

A sequential model with a couple of layers is built, compiled, and trained with the bottleneck features and can be implemented using the code given as follows:

```
model = tf.keras.models.Sequential()
model.add(tf.keras.layers.Flatten(input_shape=train_bottleneck_features.sha
pe[1:]))
model.add(tf.keras.layers.Dense(1024, activation='relu'))
model.add(tf.keras.layers.Dropout(0.3))
model.add(tf.keras.layers.Dense(1, activation='softmax'))
model.compile(loss=tf.keras.losses.categorical_crossentropy,
              optimizer=tf.keras.optimizers.Adam(),
              metrics=['accuracy'])
```

These bottleneck features are trained with the model using the code shown as follows:

```
model.fit(
    train_bottleneck_features,
    train_labels,
    batch_size=batch_size,
    epochs=epochs,
    validation_data=(test_bottleneck_features, test_labels))
```

This gives a different approach to training the model and is useful when the training data is low. This is often a faster method to train a model. Only the final activations of the pre-trained model are used to adapt to the new task. This idea can be extended to fine-tune several layers as shown next:

Fine-tuning several layers in deep learning

A pre-trained model can be loaded and only a few layers can be trained. This approach works better when the given problem is very different from the images that the model is trained upon. **Fine-tuning** is a common practice in deep learning. This gives advantages when the dataset is smaller. The optimization also can be obtained faster.

Training a deep network on a small dataset results in overfitting. This kind of overfitting can also be avoided using the fine-tuning procedure. The model trained on a bigger dataset should be also similar, as we are hoping that the activations and features are similar to the smaller dataset. You can start with the stored weights path as show below:

```
top_model_weights_path = 'fc_model.h5'
```

Load the **Visual Geometry Group (VGG)** model and set the initial layers to be non-trainable. The VGG model will be covered in detail in the following section. For now, consider VGG as a big deep learning model that works well on image data. Replace the fully connected layers with new trainable layers using the code given as follows:

```
model = tf.keras.applications.VGG16(include_top=False)
```

A small two-layer feedforward network can be built on top of the VGG model with usually hidden units, activations, and dropout as follows:

```
model_fine_tune = tf.keras.models.Sequential()
model_fine_tune.add(tf.keras.layers.Flatten(input_shape=model.output_shape)
)
model_fine_tune.add(tf.keras.layers.Dense(256, activation='relu'))
model_fine_tune.add(tf.keras.layers.Dropout(0.5))
model_fine_tune.add(tf.keras.layers.Dense(no_classes,
activation='softmax'))
```

The top model has also to be loaded with weights that are already fully trained. The top model can then be added to the convolutional base:

```
model_fine_tune.load_weights(top_model_weights_path)
model.add(model_fine_tune)
```

We can set the top 25 layers to be non-trainable up to the last convolution block so that their weights will be not be updated. Only the rest of the layers will be updated:

```
for vgg_layer in model.layers[:25]:
    vgg_layer.trainable = False
```

Compile the model with the gradient descent optimizer at a slow learning rate with a magnitude of order of 4:

```
model.compile(loss='binary_crossentropy',
              optimizer=tf.keras.optimizers.SGD(lr=1e-4, momentum=0.9),
              metrics=['accuracy'])
```

We can combine the augmentation techniques that were covered earlier with shear, zoom, and flip. The generator can be added with flow from the directory with both the train and validation datasets. Now the model can be fine-tuned combined with data augmentation. This way of training gives a better accuracy than all the previous methods. The following is a guide for transfer learning:

Data Size	Similar Dataset	Different Dataset
Smaller data	Fine-tune the output layers	Fine-tune the deeper layer
Bigger data	Fine-tune the whole model	Train from scratch

Depending on the data size, the number of layers to fine-tune can be determined. The less data there is, the lesser the number of layers to fine-tune. We have seen how to improve the accuracy of the model using transfer learning techniques.

Developing real-world applications

Recognizing cats and dogs is a cool problem but less likely a problem of importance. Real-world applications of image classification used in products may be different. You may have different data, targets, and so on. In this section, you will learn the tips and tricks to tackle such different settings. The factors that should be considered when approaching a new problem are as follows:

- The number of targets. Is it a 10 class problem or 10,000 class problem?
- How vast is the intra-class variance? For example, does the different type of cats have to be identified under one class label?
- How vast is the inter-class variance? For example, do the different cats have to be identified?
- How big is the data?
- How balanced is the data?
- Is there already a model that is trained with a lot of images?
- What is the requisite for deployment inference time and model size? Is it 50 milliseconds on an iPhone or 10 milliseconds on Google Cloud Platform? How much RAM can be consumed to store the model?

Try to answer these questions when approaching an image classification problem. Based on the answers, you can design the training architecture and improve the accuracy as described in the next section.

Choosing the right model

There are a lot of options for architectures. Based on the flexibility of deployment, you can choose the model. Remember that convolution is smaller and slower, but dense layers are bigger and faster. There is a trade-off between size, runtime, and accuracy. It is advisable to test out all the architectures before the final decision. Some models may work better than others, based on the application. You can reduce the input size to make the inference faster. Architectures can be selected based on the metrics as described in the following section.

Tackling the underfitting and overfitting scenarios

The model may be sometimes too big or too small for the problem. This could be classified as underfitting or overfitting, respectively. Underfitting happens when the model is too small and can be measured when training accuracy is less. Overfitting happens when the model is too big and there is a large gap between training and testing accuracies. Underfitting can be solved by the following methods:

- Getting more data
- Trying out a bigger model
- If the data is small, try transfer learning techniques or do data augmentation

Overfitting can be solved by the following methods:

- Regularizing using techniques such as dropout and batch normalization
- Augmenting the dataset

Always watch out for loss. The loss should be decreasing over iterations. If the loss is not decreasing, it signals that training has stopped. One solution is to try out a different optimizer. Class imbalance can be dealt with by weighting the loss function. Always use **TensorBoard** to watch the summaries. It is difficult to estimate how much data is needed. This section is the best lesson on training any deep learning models. Next, we will cover some application-specific guidance.

Gender and age detection from face

Applications may require gender and age detection from a face. The face image can be obtained by face detectors. The cropped images of faces can be supplied as training data, and the similar cropped face should be given for inference. Based on the required inference time, OpenCV, or CNN face detectors can be selected. For training, Inception or ResNet can be used. If the required inference time is much less because it is a video, it's better to use three convolutions followed by two fully connected layers. Note that there is usually a huge class imbalance in age datasets, hence using a different metric like precision and recall will be helpful.

Fine-tuning apparel models

Fine-tuning of apparel models is a good choice. Having multiple softmax layers that classify attributes will be useful here. The attributes could be a pattern, color, and so on.

Brand safety

Training bottleneck layers with **Support Vector Machine (SVM)** is a good option as the images can be quite different among classes. This is typically used for content moderation to help avoid images that are explicit. You have learned how to approach new problems in image classification.

Summary

We have covered basic, yet useful models for training classification tasks. We saw a simple model for an MNIST dataset with both Keras and TensorFlow APIs. We also saw how to utilize TensorBoard for watching the training process. Then, we discussed state-of-the-art architectures with some specific applications. Several ways to increase the accuracy such as data augmentation, training on bottleneck layers, and fine-tuning a pre-trained model were also covered. Tips and tricks to train models for new models were also presented.

In the next chapter, we will see how to visualize the deep learning models. We will also deploy the trained models in this chapter for inference. We will also see how to use the trained layers for the application of an image search through an application. Then, we will understand the concept of autoencoders and use it for the dimensionality of features.

3
Image Retrieval

Deep learning can also be called **representation learning** because the features or representations in the model are learned during training. The **visual features** generated during the training process in the hidden layers can be used for computing a distance metric. These models learn how to detect edges, patterns, and so on at various layers, depending on the classification task. In this chapter, we will look at the following:

- How to extract features from a model that was trained for classification
- How to use TensorFlow Serving for faster inference in production systems
- How to compute similarity between a query image and the set of targets using those features
- Using the classification model for ranking
- How to increase the speed of the retrieval system
- Looking at the architecture of the system as a whole
- Learning a compact descriptor when the target images are too many, using autoencoder
- Training a denoising autoencoder

Understanding visual features

Deep learning models are often criticized for not being interpretable. A neural network-based model is often considered to be like a black box because it's difficult for humans to reason out the working of a deep learning model. The transformations of an image over layers by deep learning models are non-linear due to activation functions, so cannot be visualized easily. There are methods that have been developed to tackle the criticism of the non-interpretability by visualizing the layers of the deep network. In this section, we will look at the attempts to visualize the deep layers in an effort to understand how a model works.

Visualization can be done using the activation and gradient of the model. The activation can be visualized using the following techniques:

- **Nearest neighbour**: A layer activation of an image can be taken and the nearest images of that activation can be seen together.
- **Dimensionality reduction**: The dimension of the activation can be reduced by **principal component analysis** (**PCA**) or **t-Distributed Stochastic Neighbor Embedding** (**t-SNE**) for visualizing in two or three dimensions. PCA reduces the dimension by projecting the values in the direction of maximum variance. t-SNE reduces the dimension by mapping the closest points to three dimensions. The use of dimensionality reduction and its techniques are out of the scope of this book. You are advised to refer to basic machine learning material to learn more about dimensionality reduction.

  Wikipedia is a good source for understanding dimensionality reduction techniques. Here are a few links that you can refer to:

  - https://en.wikipedia.org/wiki/Dimensionality_reduction
  - https://en.wikipedia.org/wiki/Principal_component_analysis
  - https://en.wikipedia.org/wiki/T-distributed_stochastic_neighbor_embedding
  - https://en.wikipedia.org/wiki/Locality-sensitive_hashing

- **Maximal patches**: One neuron is activated and the corresponding patch with maximum activation is captured.
- **Occlusion**: The images are occluded (obstructed) at various positions and the activation is shown as heat maps to understand what portions of the images are important.

In the following sections, we will see how to implement the visualization of these features.

Visualizing activation of deep learning models

Any model architecture can be visualized with the filters of any layer. Only the initial layers are comprehensible using the technique. The last layer is useful for the nearest neighbor approach. The `ImageNet` dataset, when arranged with nearest neighbors, looks as follows:

Looking at this image, you can see that the same objects appear together. One of the interesting things is that the animals such as the dog, monkey, and cheetah appear together though they are not trained under one label. Nearest neighbour visualization of the images is useful when objects are similar and hence, we can understand the model's predictions. This last layer can also be visualized by dimensionality reduction techniques, such as principal component analysis and t-SNE. We will see the implementation for visualization using dimensionality reduction in the next section.

Embedding visualization

The embedding layer, which is the pre-final layer, can be visualized in two or three dimensions using TensorBoard. The code snippets in this section are assumed to come after the convolution neural network model trained in the image classification chapter. First, we need a metadata file that is a tab separated file. Every line of the metadata file should have the labels of the images that are going to be visualized. A new variable is required for storing the embedding that is defined between session creation and initialization, as shown in the following code:

```
no_embedding_data = 1000
embedding_variable = tf.Variable(tf.stack(
    mnist.test.images[:no_embedding_data], axis=0), trainable=False)
```

We will take MNIST test data and create a metadata file for visualization, as shown here:

```
metadata_path = '/tmp/train/metadata.tsv'

with open(metadata_path, 'w') as metadata_file:
  for i in range(no_embedding_data):
  metadata_file.write('{}\n'.format(
  np.nonzero(mnist.test.labels[::1])[1:][0][i]))
```

The embedding variable should be made non-trainable by setting the parameter as shown in the preceding code. Next, the projector config has to be defined. It has to have a `tensor_name` which is the embedding variable name, the path to the metadata file, and a sprite image. A sprite image is one image with small images to denote the labels to be visualized with the embeddings. Here is the code for the definition of the projection of the embedding:

```
from tensorflow.contrib.tensorboard.plugins import projector
projector_config = projector.ProjectorConfig()
embedding_projection = projector_config.embeddings.add()
embedding_projection.tensor_name = embedding_variable.name
embedding_projection.metadata_path = metadata_path
```

```
embedding_projection.sprite.image_path = os.path.join(work_dir +
'/mnist_10k_sprite.png')
embedding_projection.sprite.single_image_dim.extend([28, 28])
```

The sprite image dimension has to be specified. Then the projector can be used to visualize the embedding with the summary writer and the configuration, as shown in the following code:

```
projector.visualize_embeddings(train_summary_writer, projector_config)
tf.train.Saver().save(session, '/tmp/train/model.ckpt', global_step=1)
```

Then the model is saved with the session. Then go to TensorBoard to see the following visualization:

TensorBoard illustrating the output of the code

You have to select the **T-SNE** and **color by** buttons, as shown in the screenshot, to get similar visualization. You can see how digits appear together. This visualization is very useful for the inspection of data and the embedding's that are trained. This is yet another powerful feature of TensorBoard. In the next section, we will implement guided backpropagation for visualization.

Guided backpropagation

The visualization of features directly can be less informative. Hence, we use the training procedure of backpropagation to activate the filters for better visualization. Since we pick what neurons are to be activated for backpropagation, it is called guided backpropagation. In this section, we will implement the guided backpropagation to visualize the features.

We will define the size and load the VGG model, as shown here:

```
image_width, image_height = 128, 128
vgg_model = tf.keras.applications.vgg16.VGG16(include_top=False)
```

The layers are made of a dictionary with layer names as keys, and the layer from the model with weights as the key value for ease of access. Now we will take a first convolution layer from the fifth block, `block5_conv1` for computing the visualization. The input and output are defined here:

```
input_image = vgg_model.input
vgg_layer_dict = dict([(vgg_layer.name, vgg_layer) for vgg_layer in
vgg_model.layers[1:]])
vgg_layer_output = vgg_layer_dict['block5_conv1'].output
```

We have to define the loss function. The loss function will maximize the activation of a particular layer. This is a gradient ascent process rather than the usual gradient descent as we are trying to maximize the loss function. For gradient ascent, it's important to smoothen the gradient. So we smoothen the gradient in this case by normalizing the pixel gradients. This loss function converges rather quickly.

The output of the image should be normalized to visualize it back, gradient ascent is used in an optimization process to get the maxima of a function. Now we can start the gradient ascent optimization by defining the evaluator and gradients, as shown next. Now the loss function has to be defined and gradients have to be computed. The iterator computes the loss and gradient values over iterations as shown:

```
filters = []
for filter_idx in range(20):
```

```
loss = tf.keras.backend.mean(vgg_layer_output[:, :, :, filter_idx])
gradients = tf.keras.backend.gradients(loss, input_image)[0]
gradient_mean_square =
tf.keras.backend.mean(tf.keras.backend.square(gradients))
gradients /= (tf.keras.backend.sqrt(gradient_mean_square) + 1e-5)
evaluator = tf.keras.backend.function([input_image], [loss, gradients])
```

The input is a random grey image with some noise added to it. A random image is generated and scaling is done, as shown here.

```
gradient_ascent_step = 1.
input_image_data = np.random.random((1, image_width, image_height, 3))
input_image_data = (input_image_data - 0.5) * 20 + 128
```

The optimization of the loss function is started now, and for some filters, the loss values may be 0 which should be ignored, as shown here:

```
for i in range(20):
    loss_value, gradient_values = evaluator([input_image_data])
    input_image_data += gradient_values * gradient_ascent_step
    # print('Loss :', loss_value)
    if loss_value <= 0.:
        break
```

After this optimization, normalization is done with mean subtraction and adjusting the standard deviation. Then, the filters can be scaled back and clipped to their gradient values, as shown here:

```
if loss_value > 0:
    filter = input_image_data[0]
    filter -= filter.mean()
    filter /= (filter.std() + 1e-5)
    filter *= 0.1
    filter += 0.5
    filter = np.clip(filter, 0, 1)
    filter *= 255
    filter = np.clip(filter, 0, 255).astype('uint8')
    filters.append((filter, loss_value))
```

These filters are randomly picked and are visualized here:

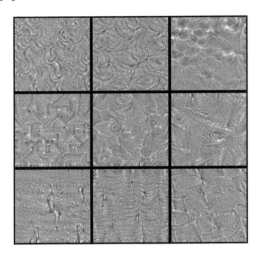

The code to stitch the images and produce an output as shown is available along with the code bundles. The visualization becomes complicated over later layers because the receptive field of the convents becomes bigger. Some filters look similar but only rotated. The hierarchy of visualization can be clearly seen in this case as shown by Zeiler et al. (https://arxiv.org/pdf/1412.6572.pdf). Direct visualization of different layers is shown in the following image:

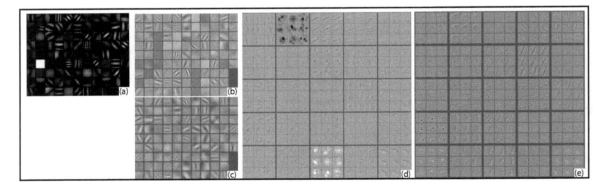

Reproduced with permission from Zeiler et al.

The first two layers look like edge and corner detectors. Gabor-like filters only appear in the third layer. Gabor filters are linear and traditionally used for texture analysis. We have seen the visualization of features directly and by guided backpropagation. Next, we will see how to implement DeepDream for visualization.

The DeepDream

The neuron activations can be amplified at some layer in the network rather than synthesizing the image. This concept of amplifying the original image to see the effect of features is called **DeepDream**. The steps for creating the DeepDream are:

1. Take an image and pick a layer from CNN.
2. Take the activations at a particular layer.
3. Modify the gradient such that the gradient and activations are equal.
4. Compute the gradients of the image and backpropagate.
5. The image has to be jittered and normalized using regularization.
6. The pixel values should be clipped.
7. Multi-scale processing of the image is done for the effect of fractal.

Let's start by importing the relevant packages:

```
import os
import numpy as np
import PIL.Image
import urllib.request
from tensorflow.python.platform import gfile
import zipfile
```

The inception model is pre-trained on the `Imagenet` dataset and the model files provided by Google. We can download that model and use it for this example. The ZIP archive of the model files are downloaded and extracted in a folder, as shown here:

```
model_url =
'https://storage.googleapis.com/download.tensorflow.org/models/inception5h.
zip'

file_name = model_url.split('/')[-1]

file_path = os.path.join(work_dir, file_name)

if not os.path.exists(file_path):
    file_path, _ = urllib.request.urlretrieve(model_url, file_path)
```

```
zip_handle = zipfile.ZipFile(file_path, 'r')
zip_handle.extractall(work_dir)
zip_handle.close()
```

These commands should have created three new files in the working directory. This pre-trained model can be loaded into the session, as shown here:

```
graph = tf.Graph()
session = tf.InteractiveSession(graph=graph)
model_path = os.path.join(work_dir, 'tensorflow_inception_graph.pb')
with gfile.FastGFile(model_path, 'rb') as f:
    graph_defnition = tf.GraphDef()
    graph_defnition.ParseFromString(f.read())
```

A session is started with the initialization of a graph. Then the graph definition of the model downloaded is loaded into the memory. The `ImageNet` mean has to be subtracted from the input as shown next, as a preprocessing step. The preprocessed image is then fed to the graph as shown:

```
input_placeholder = tf.placeholder(np.float32, name='input')
imagenet_mean_value = 117.0
preprocessed_input = tf.expand_dims(input_placeholder-imagenet_mean_value,
0)
tf.import_graph_def(graph_defnition, {'input': preprocessed_input})
```

Now the session and graph are ready for inference. A `resize_image` function will be required with bilinear interpolation. A `resize` function method can be added that resizes the image with a TensorFlow session, as shown here:

```
def resize_image(image, size):
    resize_placeholder = tf.placeholder(tf.float32)
    resize_placeholder_expanded = tf.expand_dims(resize_placeholder, 0)
    resized_image = tf.image.resize_bilinear(resize_placeholder_expanded,
size)[0, :, :, :]
    return session.run(resized_image, feed_dict={resize_placeholder:
image})
```

An image from the working directory can be loaded into the memory and converted to float value, as shown here:

```
image_name = 'mountain.jpg'
image = PIL.Image.open(image_name)
image = np.float32(image)
```

The image that is loaded is shown here, for your reference:

The number of octaves, size, and scale of the scale space are defined here:

```
no_octave = 4
scale = 1.4
window_size = 51
```

These values work well for the example shown here and hence, require tuning for other images based on their size. A layer can be selected for dreaming and the average mean of that layer will be the `objective` function, as shown here:

```
score = tf.reduce_mean(objective_fn)
gradients = tf.gradients(score, input_placeholder)[0]
```

The gradient of the images is computed for optimization. The octave images can be computed by resizing the image to various scales and finding the difference, as shown:

```
octave_images = []
for i in range(no_octave - 1):
    image_height_width = image.shape[:2]
    scaled_image = resize_image(image,
np.int32(np.float32(image_height_width) / scale))
```

```
        image_difference = image - resize_image(scaled_image,
image_height_width)
        image = scaled_image
        octave_images.append(image_difference)
```

Now the optimization can be run using all the octave images. The window is slid across the image, computing the gradients activation to create the dream, as shown here:

```
for octave_idx in range(no_octave):
    if octave_idx > 0:
        image_difference = octave_images[-octave_idx]
        image = resize_image(image, image_difference.shape[:2]) +
image_difference

    for i in range(10):
        image_heigth, image_width = image.shape[:2]
        sx, sy = np.random.randint(window_size, size=2)
        shifted_image = np.roll(np.roll(image, sx, 1), sy, 0)
        gradient_values = np.zeros_like(image)

        for y in range(0, max(image_heigth - window_size // 2,
window_size), window_size):
            for x in range(0, max(image_width - window_size // 2,
window_size), window_size):
                sub = shifted_image[y:y + window_size, x:x + window_size]
                gradient_windows = session.run(gradients,
{input_placeholder: sub})
                gradient_values[y:y + window_size, x:x + window_size] =
gradient_windows

        gradient_windows = np.roll(np.roll(gradient_values, -sx, 1), -sy,
0)
        image += gradient_windows * (1.5 / (np.abs(gradient_windows).mean()
+ 1e-7))
```

Now the optimization to create the DeepDream is completed and can be saved as shown, by clipping the values:

```
image /= 255.0
image = np.uint8(np.clip(image, 0, 1) * 255)
PIL.Image.fromarray(image).save('dream_' + image_name, 'jpeg')
```

In this section, we have seen the procedure to create the DeepDream. The result is shown here:

As we can see, dog slugs are activated everywhere. You can try various other layers and see the results. These results can be used for artistic purposes. Similarly, other layers can be activated to produce different artifacts. In the next section, we will see some adversarial examples that can fool deep learning models.

Adversarial examples

The image classification algorithms have reached human-level accuracy on several datasets. But they can be easily fooled by adversarial examples. Adversarial examples are synthetic images that fool a model to produce the outcome that is needed. Take any image and choose a random target class that is incorrect. This image can be modified with noise until the network is fooled as show by Goodfellow et al. (`https://arxiv.org/pdf/1412.6572.pdf`). An example of an adversarial attack on the model is shown here:

Reproduced with permission from Goodfellow et al.

In this figure, an image is shown on the left with 58% confidence of a particular label. The left image, when combined with noise which is shown in the middle, forms the image on the right side. For a human, the image with noise stills looks the same. But the image with noise is predicted with a different label with 97% confidence. High confidence is assigned to a particular example, despite the image having a very different object. This is a problem with deep learning models and hence, you should understand where this is applicable:

- The adversarial example can even be generated without the access to the models. You can train your own model, generate an adversarial example and can still fool a different model.
- This occurs rarely in practice but it becomes a true problem when someone tries to fool a system for spamming or crashing.
- All machine learning models are susceptible to this problem, not just deep learning models.

You should understand the consequences of deploying a deep learning model on a safety critical system, considering the adversarial examples. In the next section, we will see how to utilize TensorFlow Serving to get a faster inference.

Model inference

Any new data can be passed to the model to get the results. This process of getting the classification results or features from an image is termed as **inference**. Training and inference usually happen on different computers and at different times. We will learn about storing the model, running the inference, and using TensorFlow Serving as the server with good latency and throughput.

Exporting a model

The model after training has to be exported and saved. The weights, biases, and the graph are stored for inference. We will train an MNIST model and store it. Start with defining the constants that are required, using the following code:

```
work_dir = '/tmp'
model_version = 9
training_iteration = 1000
input_size = 784
no_classes = 10
batch_size = 100
total_batches = 200
```

The `model_version` can be an integer to specify which model we want to export for serving. The `feature config` is stored as a dictionary with placeholder names and their corresponding datatype. The prediction classes and their labels should be mapped. The identity placeholder can be used with the API:

```
tf_example = tf.parse_example(tf.placeholder(tf.string, name='tf_example'),
                              {'x': tf.FixedLenFeature(shape=[784],
dtype=tf.float32), })
x_input = tf.identity(tf_example['x'], name='x')
```

A simple classifier can be defined with weights, biases, logits, and an optimizer, using the following code:

```
y_input = tf.placeholder(tf.float32, shape=[None, no_classes])
weights = tf.Variable(tf.random_normal([input_size, no_classes]))
bias = tf.Variable(tf.random_normal([no_classes]))
logits = tf.matmul(x_input, weights) + bias
softmax_cross_entropy =
tf.nn.softmax_cross_entropy_with_logits(labels=y_input, logits=logits)
loss_operation = tf.reduce_mean(softmax_cross_entropy)
optimiser = tf.train.GradientDescentOptimizer(0.5).minimize(loss_operation)
```

Train the model as shown in the following code:

```
mnist = input_data.read_data_sets('MNIST_data', one_hot=True)
for batch_no in range(total_batches):
    mnist_batch = mnist.train.next_batch(batch_size)
    _, loss_value = session.run([optimiser, loss_operation], feed_dict={
        x_input: mnist_batch[0],
        y_input: mnist_batch[1]
    })
    print(loss_value)
```

Define the prediction signature, and export the model. Save the model to a persistent storage so that it can be used for inference at a later point in time. This exports the data by deserialization and stores it in a format that can be understood by different systems. Multiple graphs with different variables and placeholders can be used for exporting. It also supports `signature_defs` and assets. The `signature_defs` have the inputs and outputs specified because input and output will be accessed from the external clients. Assets are non-graph components that will be utilized for the inference, such as vocabulary and so on.

The classification signature uses access to the classification API of TensorFlow. An input is compulsory and there are two optional outputs (prediction classes and prediction probabilities), with at least one being compulsory. The prediction signature offers flexibility with the number of inputs and outputs. Multiple outputs can be defined and explicitly queried from the client side. The `signature_def` is shown here:

```
signature_def = (
    tf.saved_model.signature_def_utils.build_signature_def(
        inputs={'x': tf.saved_model.utils.build_tensor_info(x_input)},
        outputs={'y': tf.saved_model.utils.build_tensor_info(y_input)},
        method_name="tensorflow/serving/predict"))
```

Finally, add the metagraph and variables to the builder with the prediction signature:

```
model_path = os.path.join(work_dir, str(model_version))
saved_model_builder = tf.saved_model.builder.SavedModelBuilder(model_path)
saved_model_builder.add_meta_graph_and_variables(
    session, [tf.saved_model.tag_constants.SERVING],
    signature_def_map={
        'prediction': signature_def
    },
    legacy_init_op=tf.group(tf.tables_initializer(),
name='legacy_init_op'))
saved_model_builder.save()
```

The builder is saved and ready to be consumed by the server. The shown example is applicable to any model and can be used for exporting. In the next section, we will serve and query the exported model.

Serving the trained model

The model that is exported in the previous section can be served via TensorFlow Serving using the following command:

```
tensorflow_model_server --port=9000 --model_name=mnist --
model_base_path=/tmp/mnist_model/
```

The `model_base_path` points to the directory of the exported model. The server can now be tested with the client. Note that this is not an HTTP server, and hence, a client as shown here, is needed instead of an HTTP client. Import the required libraries:

```
from grpc.beta import implementations
import numpy
import tensorflow as tf
from tensorflow.examples.tutorials.mnist import input_data
```

```
from tensorflow_serving.apis import predict_pb2
from tensorflow_serving.apis import prediction_service_pb2
```

Add the constants for concurrency, the number of tests, and working directory. A class is defined for counting the results returned. A **Remote Procedure Call (RPC)** callback is defined with a counter for counting the predictions, as shown here:

```
concurrency = 1
num_tests = 100
host = ''
port = 8000
work_dir = '/tmp'


def _create_rpc_callback():
  def _callback(result):
      response = numpy.array(
        result.result().outputs['y'].float_val)
      prediction = numpy.argmax(response)
      print(prediction)
  return _callback
```

Modify the host and port according to your requirements. The _callback method defines the steps required when the response comes back from the server. In this case, the maximum of the probabilities is computed. Run the inference by calling the server:

```
test_data_set = mnist.test
test_image = mnist.test.images[0]

predict_request = predict_pb2.PredictRequest()
predict_request.model_spec.name = 'mnist'
predict_request.model_spec.signature_name = 'prediction'

predict_channel = implementations.insecure_channel(host, int(port))
predict_stub =
prediction_service_pb2.beta_create_PredictionService_stub(predict_channel)

predict_request.inputs['x'].CopyFrom(
    tf.contrib.util.make_tensor_proto(test_image, shape=[1,
test_image.size]))
result = predict_stub.Predict.future(predict_request, 3.0)
result.add_done_callback(
    _create_rpc_callback())
```

Call the inference repeatedly to gauge the accuracy, latency, and throughput. The inference error rate should be around 90%, and the concurrency should be great. The export and client methods can be used together for any model to obtain the results and features from the model. In the next section, we will build the retrieval pipeline.

Content-based image retrieval

The technique of **Content-based Image Retrieval** (**CBIR**) takes a query image as the input and ranks images from a database of target images, producing the output. CBIR is an image to image search engine with a specific goal. A database of target images is required for retrieval. The target images with the minimum distance from the query image are returned. We can use the image directly for similarity, but the problems are as follows:

- The image is of huge dimensions
- There is a lot of redundancy in pixels
- A pixel doesn't carry the semantic information

So, we train a model for object classification and use the features from the model for retrieval. Then we pass the query image and database of targets through the same model to get the features. The models can also be called **encoders** as they encode the information about the images for the particular task. Encoders should be able to capture global and local features. We can use the models that we studied in the image classification chapter, trained for a classification task. The searching of the image may take a lot of time, as a brute-force or linear scan is slow. Hence, some methods for faster retrieval are required. Here are some methods for faster matching:

- **Locality sensitive hashing** (**LSH**): LSH projects the features to their subspace and can give a candidate a list and do a fine-feature ranking later. This is also a dimensionality reduction technique such as PCA and t-SNE which we covered earlier in the chapter. This has feature buckets in lower dimensions.
- **Multi-index hashing**: This method hashes the features and it is like pigeonhole fitting making it faster. It uses hamming distance to make the computation faster. Hamming distance is nothing but the number of location differences of the numbers when expressed in binary.

These methods are faster, need lesser memory, with the trade-off being accuracy. These methods also don't capture the semantic difference. The matches results can be re-ranked to get better results based on the query. Re-ranking can improve the results by reordering the returned target images. Re-ranking may use one of the following techniques:

- **Geometric verification**: This method matches the geometries and target images with only similar geometries returned.
- **Query expansion**: This expands the list of target images and searches them exhaustively.
- **Relevance feedback**: This method gets the feedback from the use and returns the results. Based on the user input, the re-ranking will be done.

These techniques are well developed for text and can be used for images. In this chapter, we will focus on extracting features and use them for CBIR. In the next section, we will learn how to do model inference.

Building the retrieval pipeline

The sequence of steps to get the best matches from target images for a query image is called the **retrieval pipeline**. The retrieval pipeline has multiple steps or components. The features of the image database have to be extracted offline and stored in a database. For every query image, the feature has to be extracted and similarity has to be computed across all of the target images. Then the images can be ranked for final output. The retrieval pipeline is shown here:

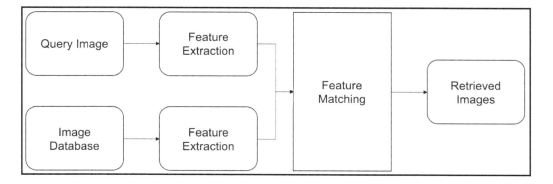

The feature extraction step has to be fast, for which TensorFlow Serving can be used. You can choose which features to use depending on the application. For example, initial layers can be used when texture-based matching is required, later layers can be used when it has to be matched at an object level. In the next section, we will see how to extract features from a pre-trained inception model.

Extracting bottleneck features for an image

Bottleneck features are the values computed in the pre-classification layer. In this section, we will see how to extract the bottleneck features from a pre-trained model using TensorFlow. Let's start by importing the required libraries, using the following code:

```
import os
import urllib.request
from tensorflow.python.platform import gfile
import tarfile
```

Then, we need to download the pre-trained model with the graph definition and its weights. TensorFlow has trained a model on the `ImageNet` dataset using inception architecture and provided the model. We will download this model and unzip it into a local folder, using the following code:

```
model_url =
'http://download.tensorflow.org/models/image/imagenet/inception-2015-12-05.
tgz'
file_name = model_url.split('/')[-1]
file_path = os.path.join(work_dir, file_name)

if not os.path.exists(file_path):
    file_path, _ = urllib.request.urlretrieve(model_url, file_path)
tarfile.open(file_path, 'r:gz').extractall(work_dir)
```

This created a folder and downloaded the model, only when it does not exist. If the code is executed repeatedly, the model won't be downloaded every time. The graph is stored in a **Protocol Buffers** (**protobuf**) format in a file. This has to be read as a string and passed to the `tf.GraphDef()` object to bring it into memory:

```
model_path = os.path.join(work_dir, 'classify_image_graph_def.pb')
with gfile.FastGFile(model_path, 'rb') as f:
    graph_defnition = tf.GraphDef()
    graph_defnition.ParseFromString(f.read())
```

In the inception model, the bottleneck layer is named `pool_3/_reshape:0`, and the layer is of 2,048 dimensions. The input placeholder name is `DecodeJpeg/contents:0`, and the resize tensor name is `ResizeBilinear:0`. We can import the graph definition using `tf.import_graph_def` with the required return tensors for further operations:

```
bottleneck, image, resized_input = (
    tf.import_graph_def(
        graph_defnition,
        name='',
        return_elements=['pool_3/_reshape:0',
                        'DecodeJpeg/contents:0',
                        'ResizeBilinear:0'])
)
```

Take a query and target image and load it in the memory. The `gfile` function provides a faster way to load the image into the memory.

```
query_image_path = os.path.join(work_dir, 'cat.1000.jpg')
query_image = gfile.FastGFile(query_image_path, 'rb').read()
target_image_path = os.path.join(work_dir, 'cat.1001.jpg')
target_image = gfile.FastGFile(target_image_path, 'rb').read()
```

Let us define a function that extracts the bottleneck feature from an image, using the `session` and image:

```
def get_bottleneck_data(session, image_data):
    bottleneck_data = session.run(bottleneck, {image: image_data})
    bottleneck_data = np.squeeze(bottleneck_data)
    return bottleneck_data
```

Initiate the session, and pass the image to run the forward inference to get the bottleneck values from the pre-trained model:

```
query_feature = get_bottleneck_data(session, query_image)
print(query_feature)
target_feature = get_bottleneck_data(session, target_image)
print(target_feature)
```

Running the above code should print as shown here:

```
[ 0.55705792 0.36785451 1.06618118 ..., 0.6011821 0.36407694
  0.0996572 ]
[ 0.30421323 0.0926369 0.26213276 ..., 0.72273785 0.30847171
  0.08719242]
```

This procedure of computing the features can be scaled for more target images. Using the values, the similarity can be computed between the query image and target database as described in the following section.

Computing similarity between query image and target database

NumPy's `linalg.norm` is useful for computing the **Euclidean distance**. The similarity between the query image and target database can be computed between the images by calculating the Euclidean distances between the features as shown here:

```
dist = np.linalg.norm(np.asarray(query_feature) -
np.asarray(target_feature))
print(dist)
```

Running this command should print the following:

```
16.9965
```

This is the metric that can be used for similarity calculation. The smaller the Euclidean distance between the query and the target image is, the more similar the images are. Hence, computing the Euclidean distance is a measurement of similarity. Using the features for computing the Euclidean distance is based on the assumption that the features are learned during the training of the model. Scaling this computation for millions of images is not efficient. In a production system, it is expected to return the results in milliseconds. In the next section, we will see how to make this retrieval efficient.

Efficient retrieval

The retrieval can be slow because it's a brute-force method. Matching can be made faster using approximate nearest neighbor. The curse of dimensionality also kicks in, as shown in the following figure:

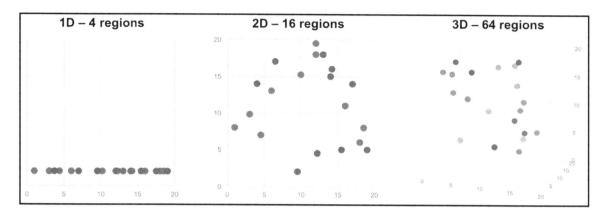

With every increasing dimension, complexity increases as the complexity from two dimensions to three dimensions. The computation of the distance also becomes slower. To make the distance search faster, we will discuss an approximate method in the next section.

Matching faster using approximate nearest neighbour

Approximate nearest neighbour oh yeah (**ANNOY**) is a method for faster nearest neighbour search. ANNOY builds trees by random projections. The tree structure makes it easier to find the closest matches. You can create an `ANNOYIndex` for faster retrieval as shown here:

```
def create_annoy(target_features):
    t = AnnoyIndex(layer_dimension)
    for idx, target_feature in enumerate(target_features):
        t.add_item(idx, target_feature)
    t.build(10)
    t.save(os.path.join(work_dir, 'annoy.ann'))

create_annoy(target_features)
```

The dimension of the features is required for creating the index. Then the items are added to the index and the tree is built. The bigger the number of trees, the more accurate the results will be with a trade-off of time and space complexity. The index can be created and loaded into the memory. The ANNOY can be queried as shown here:

```
annoy_index = AnnoyIndex(10)
annoy_index.load(os.path.join(work_dir, 'annoy.ann'))
matches = annoy_index.get_nns_by_vector(query_feature, 20)
```

The list of matches can be used to retrieve the image details. The index of the items will be returned.

 Visit `https://github.com/spotify/annoy` for a complete implementation of ANNOY and its benchmark comparison against other approximate nearest neighbour algorithms, in terms of accuracy and speed.

Advantages of ANNOY

There are many reasons for using ANNOY. The main advantages are listed as follows:

- Has a memory-mapped data structure, hence, less intensive on RAM. The same file can be shared among multiple processes due to this.
- Multiple distances such as Manhattan, Cosine, or Euclidean can be used for computing the similarity between the query image and target database.

Autoencoders of raw images

An autoencoder is an unsupervised algorithm for generating efficient encodings. The input layer and the target output is typically the same. The layers between decrease and increase in the following fashion:

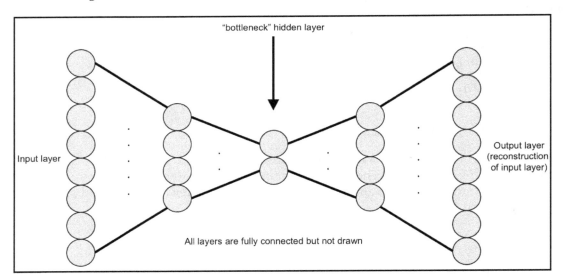

The **bottleneck** layer is the middle layer with a reduced dimension. The left side of the bottleneck layer is called **encoder** and the right side is called **decoder**. An encoder typically reduces the dimension of the data and a decoder increases the dimensions. This combination of encoder and decoder is called an autoencoder. The whole network is trained with reconstruction error. Theoretically, the bottleneck layer can be stored and the original data can be reconstructed by the decoder network. This reduces the dimensions and can be programmed easily, as shown next. Define a convolution, deconvolution, and fully connected layer, using the following code:

```
def fully_connected_layer(input_layer, units):
    return tf.layers.dense(
        input_layer,
        units=units,
        activation=tf.nn.relu
    )


def convolution_layer(input_layer, filter_size):
    return  tf.layers.conv2d(
        input_layer,
        filters=filter_size,
        kernel_initializer=tf.contrib.layers.xavier_initializer_conv2d(),
        kernel_size=3,
        strides=2
    )


def deconvolution_layer(input_layer, filter_size, activation=tf.nn.relu):
    return tf.layers.conv2d_transpose(
        input_layer,
        filters=filter_size,
        kernel_initializer=tf.contrib.layers.xavier_initializer_conv2d(),
        kernel_size=3,
        activation=activation,
        strides=2
    )
```

Define the converging encoder with five layers of convolution, as shown in the following code:

```
input_layer = tf.placeholder(tf.float32, [None, 128, 128, 3])
convolution_layer_1 = convolution_layer(input_layer, 1024)
convolution_layer_2 = convolution_layer(convolution_layer_1, 512)
convolution_layer_3 = convolution_layer(convolution_layer_2, 256)
convolution_layer_4 = convolution_layer(convolution_layer_3, 128)
convolution_layer_5 = convolution_layer(convolution_layer_4, 32)
```

Compute the bottleneck layer by flattening the fifth convolution layer. The bottleneck layer is again reshaped back fit a convolution layer, as shown here:

```
convolution_layer_5_flattened = tf.layers.flatten(convolution_layer_5)
bottleneck_layer = fully_connected_layer(convolution_layer_5_flattened, 16)
c5_shape = convolution_layer_5.get_shape().as_list()
c5f_flat_shape = convolution_layer_5_flattened.get_shape().as_list()[1]
fully_connected = fully_connected_layer(bottleneck_layer, c5f_flat_shape)
fully_connected = tf.reshape(fully_connected,
                        [-1, c5_shape[1], c5_shape[2], c5_shape[3]])
```

Compute the diverging or decoder part that can reconstruct the image, as shown in the following code:

```
deconvolution_layer_1 = deconvolution_layer(fully_connected, 128)
deconvolution_layer_2 = deconvolution_layer(deconvolution_layer_1, 256)
deconvolution_layer_3 = deconvolution_layer(deconvolution_layer_2, 512)
deconvolution_layer_4 = deconvolution_layer(deconvolution_layer_3, 1024)
deconvolution_layer_5 = deconvolution_layer(deconvolution_layer_4, 3,
                        activation=tf.nn.tanh)
```

This network is trained and it quickly converges. The bottleneck layer can be stored when passed with image features. This helps in decreasing the size of the database, which can be used for retrieval. Only the encoder part is needed for indexing the features. Autoencoder is a lossy compression algorithm. It is different from other compression algorithms because it learns the compression pattern from the data. Hence, an autoencoder model is specific to the data. An autoencoder could be combined with t-SNE for a better visualization. The bottleneck layers learned by the autoencoder might not be useful for other tasks. The size of the bottleneck layer can be larger than previous layers. In such a case of diverging and converging connections are sparse autoencoders. In the next section, we will learn another application of autoencoders.

Denoising using autoencoders

Autoencoders can also be used for image denoising. Denoising is the process of removing noise from the image. A denoising encoder can be trained in an unsupervised manner. The noise can be introduced in a normal image and the autoencoder is trained against the original images. Later, the full autoencoder can be used to produce noise-free images. In this section, we will see step-by-step instructions to denoise MNIST images. Import the required libraries and define the placeholders as shown:

```
x_input = tf.placeholder(tf.float32, shape=[None, input_size])
y_input = tf.placeholder(tf.float32, shape=[None, input_size])
```

Both `x_input` and `y_input` are of the same shape as they should be in an autoencoder. Then, define a dense layer as shown here, with the default activation as the `tanh` activation function. The method, `add_variable_summary` is imported from the image classification chapter example. The definition of the dense layer is shown here:

```
def dense_layer(input_layer, units, activation=tf.nn.tanh):
    layer = tf.layers.dense(
        inputs=input_layer,
        units=units,
        activation=activation
    )
    add_variable_summary(layer, 'dense')
    return layer
```

Next, the autoencoder layers can be defined. This autoencoder has only fully connected layers. The encoder part has three layers of reducing dimensions. The decoder part has three layers of increasing dimensions. Both the encoder and decoder are symmetrical as shown here:

```
layer_1 = dense_layer(x_input, 500)
layer_2 = dense_layer(layer_1, 250)
layer_3 = dense_layer(layer_2, 50)
layer_4 = dense_layer(layer_3, 250)
layer_5 = dense_layer(layer_4, 500)
layer_6 = dense_layer(layer_5, 784)
```

The dimensions of the hidden layers are arbitrarily chosen. Next, the `loss` and `optimiser` are defined. Here we use sigmoid instead of softmax as classification, as shown here:

```
with tf.name_scope('loss'):
    softmax_cross_entropy = tf.nn.sigmoid_cross_entropy_with_logits(
        labels=y_input, logits=layer_6)
    loss_operation = tf.reduce_mean(softmax_cross_entropy, name='loss')
    tf.summary.scalar('loss', loss_operation)

with tf.name_scope('optimiser'):
    optimiser = tf.train.AdamOptimizer().minimize(loss_operation)
```

TensorBoard offers another kind of summary called `image`, which is useful for visualizing the images. We will take the input, `layer_6` and reshape it to add it to the summary, as shown here:

```
x_input_reshaped = tf.reshape(x_input, [-1, 28, 28, 1])
tf.summary.image("noisy_images", x_input_reshaped)

y_input_reshaped = tf.reshape(y_input, [-1, 28, 28, 1])
```

```
tf.summary.image("original_images", y_input_reshaped)

layer_6_reshaped = tf.reshape(layer_6, [-1, 28, 28, 1])
tf.summary.image("reconstructed_images", layer_6_reshaped)
```

The number of images is restricted to three by default and can be changed. This is to restrict it from writing all the images to the summary folder. Next, all the summaries are merged and the graph is added to the summary writer as shown:

```
merged_summary_operation = tf.summary.merge_all()
train_summary_writer = tf.summary.FileWriter('/tmp/train', session.graph)
```

A normal random noise can be added to the image and fed as the input tensors. After the noise is added, the extra values are clipped. The target will be the original images themselves. The addition of noise and training procedure is shown here:

```
for batch_no in range(total_batches):
    mnist_batch = mnist_data.train.next_batch(batch_size)
    train_images, _ = mnist_batch[0], mnist_batch[1]
    train_images_noise = train_images + 0.2 *
np.random.normal(size=train_images.shape)
    train_images_noise = np.clip(train_images_noise, 0., 1.)
    _, merged_summary = session.run([optimiser, merged_summary_operation],
                                    feed_dict={
        x_input: train_images_noise,
        y_input: train_images,
    })
    train_summary_writer.add_summary(merged_summary, batch_no)
```

When this training is started, the results can be seen in TensorBoard. The loss is shown here:

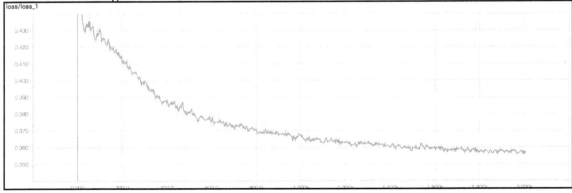

Tensorboard illustrating the output plot

The loss steadily decreases and will keep decreasing slowly over the iterations. This shows how autoencoders converge quickly. Next, three digits are displayed from the original images:

Here are the same images with noise added:

You will notice that there is significant noise and this is given as an input. Next, are the reconstructed images of the same numbers with the denoising autoencoder:

You will notice that the denoising autoencoder has done a fantastic job of removing the noise. You can run this on test images and can see the quality is maintained. For more complex datasets, you can use the convolutional neural net for better results. This example shows the power of deep learning of computer vision, given that this is trained in an unsupervised manner.

Summary

In this chapter, you have learned how to extract features from an image and use them for CBIR. You also learned how to use TensorFlow Serving to get the inference of image features. We saw how to utilize approximate nearest neighbour or faster matching rather than a linear scan. You understood how hashing may still improve the results. The idea of autoencoders was introduced, and we saw how to train smaller feature vectors for search. An example of image denoising using an autoencoder was also shown. We saw the possibility of using a bit-based comparison that can scale this up to billions of images.

In the next chapter, we will see how to train models for object detection problems. We will leverage open source models to get good accuracy and understand all the algorithms behind them. At the end, we will use all the ideas to train a pedestrian detection model.

4
Object Detection

Object detection is the act of finding the location of an object in an image. In this chapter, we will learn the techniques of object detection and implement pedestrian detection by understanding the following topics:

- Basics and the difference between localization and detection
- Various datasets and their descriptions
- Algorithms used for object localization and detection
- TensorFlow API for object detection
- Training new object detection models
- Pedestrian detection on a moving car with YOLO algorithm

Detecting objects in an image

Object detection had an explosion concerning both applications and research in recent years. Object detection is a problem of importance in computer vision. Similar to image classification tasks, deeper networks have shown better performance in detection. At present, the accuracy of these techniques is excellent. Hence it used in many applications.

Image classification labels the image as a whole. Finding the position of the object in addition to labeling the object is called **object localization**. Typically, the position of the object is defined by rectangular coordinates. Finding multiple objects in the image with rectangular coordinates is called detection. Here is an example of object detection:

The image shows four objects with bounding boxes. We will learn algorithms that can perform the task of finding the boxes. The applications are enormous in robot vision, such as self-driving cars and industrial objects. We can summarize localization and detection tasks to the following points:

- Localization detects one object in an image within a label
- Detection finds all the objects within the image along with the labels

The difference is the number of objects. In detection, there are a variable number of objects. This small difference makes a big difference when designing the architectures for the deep learning model concerning localization or detection. Next, we will see various datasets available for the tasks.

Exploring the datasets

The datasets available for object localization and detection are many. In this section, we will explore the datasets that are used by the research community to evaluate the algorithms. There are datasets with a varying number of objects, ranging from 20 to 200 annotated in these datasets, which makes object detection hard. Some datasets have too many objects in one image compared to other datasets with just one object per image. Next, we will see the datasets in detail.

ImageNet dataset

ImageNet has data for evaluating classification, localization, and detection tasks. The `Chapter 2`, *Image Classification*, discussed classification datasets in detail. Similar to classification data, there are 1,000 classes for localization tasks. The accuracy is calculated based on the top five detections. There will be at least one bounding box in all the images. There are 200 objects for detection problems with 470,000 images, with an average of 1.1 objects per image.

PASCAL VOC challenge

The PASCAL VOC challenge ran from 2005 to 2012. This challenge was considered the benchmark for object detection techniques. There are 20 classes in the dataset. The dataset has 11,530 images for training and validations with 27,450 annotations for regions of interest. The following are the twenty classes present in the dataset:

- Person: Person
- Animal: Bird, cat, cow, dog, horse, sheep
- Vehicle: Airplane, bicycle, boat, bus, car, motorbike, train
- Indoor: Bottle, chair, dining table, potted plant, sofa, tv/monitor

You can download the dataset from `http://host.robots.ox.ac.uk/pascal/VOC/voc2012/VOCtrainval_11-May-2012.tar`. There is an average of 2.4 objects per image.

COCO object detection challenge

The **Common Objects in Context** (**COCO**) dataset has 200,000 images with more than 500,000 object annotations in 80 categories. It is the most extensive publicly available object detection database. The following image has the list of objects present in the dataset:

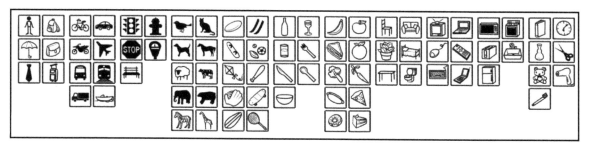

The average number of objects is 7.2 per image. These are the famous datasets for the object detection challenge. Next, we will learn how to evaluate the algorithms against these datasets.

Evaluating datasets using metrics

Metrics are essential for understanding in the context of a deep learning task. The metrics of object detection and localization are peculiar because of human annotation. The human may have annotated a box that is called **ground-truth**. The ground-truth need not be the absolute truth. Moreover, the boxes can be a few pixels different from human to human. Hence it becomes harder for the algorithm to detect the exact bounding box drawn by humans. **Intersection over Union** (IoU) is used to evaluate the localization task. **Mean Precision Average** (mAP) is used to evaluate the detection task. We will see the descriptions of the metrics in the next sections.

Intersection over Union

The IoU is the ratio of the overlapping area of **ground truth** and predicted area to the total area. Here is a visual explanation of the metric:

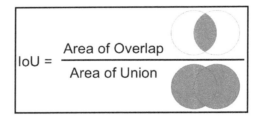

The two squares represent the bounding boxes of ground truth and predictions. The IoU is calculated as a ratio of the area of overlap to the area of the union. Here is the script to compute the IoU is given ground truth and prediction bounding boxes:

```
def calculate_iou(gt_bb, pred_bb):
    '''
    :param gt_bb: ground truth bounding box
    :param pred_bb: predicted bounding box
    '''
    gt_bb = tf.stack([
        gt_bb[:, :, :, :, 0] - gt_bb[:, :, :, :, 2] / 2.0,
        gt_bb[:, :, :, :, 1] - gt_bb[:, :, :, :, 3] / 2.0,
        gt_bb[:, :, :, :, 0] + gt_bb[:, :, :, :, 2] / 2.0,
```

```
            gt_bb[:, :, :, :, 1] + gt_bb[:, :, :, :, 3] / 2.0])
    gt_bb = tf.transpose(gt_bb, [1, 2, 3, 4, 0])
    pred_bb = tf.stack([
        pred_bb[:, :, :, :, 0] - pred_bb[:, :, :, :, 2] / 2.0,
        pred_bb[:, :, :, :, 1] - pred_bb[:, :, :, :, 3] / 2.0,
        pred_bb[:, :, :, :, 0] + pred_bb[:, :, :, :, 2] / 2.0,
        pred_bb[:, :, :, :, 1] + pred_bb[:, :, :, :, 3] / 2.0])
    pred_bb = tf.transpose(pred_bb, [1, 2, 3, 4, 0])
    area = tf.maximum(
        0.0,
        tf.minimum(gt_bb[:, :, :, :, 2:], pred_bb[:, :, :, :, 2:]) -
        tf.maximum(gt_bb[:, :, :, :, :2], pred_bb[:, :, :, :, :2]))
    intersection_area= area[:, :, :, :, 0] * area[:, :, :, :, 1]
    gt_bb_area = (gt_bb[:, :, :, :, 2] - gt_bb[:, :, :, :, 0]) * \
                 (gt_bb[:, :, :, :, 3] - gt_bb[:, :, :, :, 1])
    pred_bb_area = (pred_bb[:, :, :, :, 2] - pred_bb[:, :, :, :, 0]) * \
                   (pred_bb[:, :, :, :, 3] - pred_bb[:, :, :, :, 1])
    union_area = tf.maximum(gt_bb_area + pred_bb_area - intersection_area,
1e-10)
    iou = tf.clip_by_value(intersection_area / union_area, 0.0, 1.0)
    return iou
```

The ground truth and predicted bounding boxes are stacked together. Then the area is calculated while handling the case of negative area. The negative area could occur when bounding box coordinates are incorrect. The right side coordinates of the box many occur left to the left coordinates. Since the structure of the bounding box is not preserved, the negative area is bound to occur. The union and intersection areas are computed followed by a final IoU calculation which is the ratio of the overlapping area of **ground truth** and predicted area to the total area. The IoU calculation can be coupled with algorithms to train localization problems.

The mean average precision

The mAP is used for evaluating detection algorithms. The mAP metric is the product of precision and recall of the detected bounding boxes. The mAP value ranges from 0 to 100. The higher the number, the better it is. The mAP can be computed by calculating **average precision** (**AP**) separately for each class, then the average over the class. A detection is considered a true positive only if the mAP is above 0.5. All detections from the test images can be combined by drawing a draw precision/recall curve for each class. The final area under the curve can be used for the comparison of algorithms. The mAP is a good measure of the sensitivity of the network while not raising many false alarms. We have learned the evaluating algorithms for the datasets. Next, we will look at algorithms for a localization task.

Localizing algorithms

Localization algorithms are an extension of the materials learned in Chapter 2, *Image Classification* and Chapter 3, *Image Retrieval*. In image classification, an image is passed through several layers of a CNN (convolutional neural network). The final layer of CNN outputs the probabilistic value, belonging to each of the labels. This can be extended to localize the objects. We will see these ideas in the following sections.

Localizing objects using sliding windows

An intuitive way of localization is to predict several cropped portions of an image with an object. The cropping of the images can be done by moving a window across the image and predicting for every window. The method of moving a smaller window than the image and cropping the image according to window size is called a **sliding window**. A prediction can be made for every cropped window of the image which is called sliding window object detection.

The prediction can be done by the deep learning model trained for image classification problems with closely-cropped images. Close cropping means that only one object will be found in the whole image. The movement of the window has to be uniform across the image. Each portion of the image is passed through the model to find the classification. There are two problems with this approach.

- It can only find objects that are the same size as the window. The sliding window will miss an object if the object size is bigger than the window size. To overcome this, we will use the concept of **scale space**.
- Another problem is that moving the window over pixels may lead to missing a few objects. Moving the window over every pixel will result in a lot of extra computation hence it will slow down the system. To avoid this, we will incorporate a trick in the convolutional layers.

We will cover both these techniques in the next section.

The scale-space concept

The scale-space is the concept of using images that are of various sizes. An image is reduced to smaller size, hence bigger objects can be detected with the same-sized window. An image can be resized to some sizes with decreasing sizes. The resizing of images by removing alternative pixels or interpolation may leave some artefacts. Hence the image is smoothened and resized iteratively. The images that are obtained by smoothening and resizing are scale space.

The window is slide on every single scale for the localization of objects. Running multiple scales is equivalent to running the image with a bigger window. The computational complexity of running on multiple scales is high. Localization can be sped up by moving faster with a trade-off for accuracy. The complexity makes the solution not usable in production. The idea of the sliding window could be made efficient with a fully convolutional implementation of sliding windows.

Training a fully connected layer as a convolution layer

The problem with the sliding window is the computational complexity. The complexity is because predictions are made for every window. Deep learning features have been computed for every window for overlapping regions. This computation of features for overlapping regions in cropped windows can be reduced. The solution is to use a fully convolutional net which computes the feature only once. For understanding a fully convolutional net, let's first see how to convert a fully connected layer to a `convolution_layer`. The kernel is changed to the same size, with the same number of filters as the number of neurons. It can be repeated for other layers too. Changing the kernel size is an easier way to convert a fully connected layer to a `convolution_layer`:

```
convolution_layer_1 = convolution_layer(x_input_reshape, 64)
pooling_layer_1 = pooling_layer(convolution_layer_1)
convolution_layer_2 = convolution_layer(pooling_layer_1, 128)
pooling_layer_2 = pooling_layer(convolution_layer_2)
dense_layer_bottleneck = convolution_layer(pooling_layer_2, 1024, [5, 5])
logits = convolution_layer(dense_layer_bottleneck, no_classes, [1, 1])
logits = tf.reshape(logits, [-1, 10])
```

The dense layers are expressed as convolution layers. This idea is powerful and useful in various scenarios. We will extend this idea to express sliding window as a full convolution network.

Convolution implementation of sliding window

In this technique, instead of sliding, the final target is made into some targets required as depth and a number of boxes as the window. Sermanet et al. (`https://arxiv.org/pdf/1312.6229.pdf`) used fully convolution implementation to overcome this problem of the sliding window. Here is an illustration of such convolution implementation, of the sliding window:

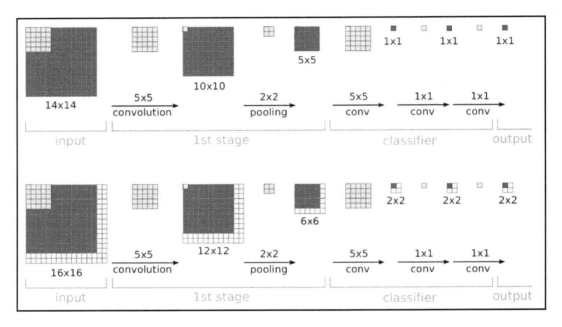

Reproduced with permission from Sermanet et al.

In the upper part of the example, normal classification is represented as a fully convolutional layer. In the lower part of the illustration, the same kernel is applied to a bigger image producing **2x2** at the end instead of 1. The final layer denotes four of the output of those bounding boxes. Having a volume for prediction improves efficiency, but the boxes still have a problem with accurate positioning. So the sliding window is not necessary, hence it solves the complexity. The aspect ratio is always changing and has to be seen at multiple scales. The bounding boxes produced by the fully convolutional method are not very accurate. The extra computations are done only for the extra region. As you can imagine, the boxes are rather restricted to the number of boxes that are trained with. Next, we will see a method to detect the bounding box positions more accurately.

Thinking about localization as a regression problem

One fundamental way to think about localization is modeling the problem as a regression problem. The bounding box is four numbers and hence can be predicted in a direct manner with a setting for regression. We will also need to predict the label, which is a classification problem.

There are different parameterizations available to define the bounding boxes. There are four numbers usually for the bounding box. One of the representations is the center of the coordinates with the height and width of the bounding box. A pre-trained model can be used by removing the fully connected layer and replacing it with a regression encoder. The regression has to be regularized with the L2 loss which performs poorly with an outlier. The L1 loss is better than L1. Swapping regression with a smoothened version of regularization is better. Fine-tuning the model gives a good accuracy, whereas training the whole network gives only a marginal performance improvement. It's a trade-off between training time and accuracy. Next, we will see different applications of regression using convolutional networks.

Applying regression to other problems

Regressing image coordinates is applicable to several other applications, such as **pose detection** and **fiducial point detection**. Pose detection is the act of finding joint locations in a human, as shown here:

In the preceding image, multiple locations such as head, neck, shoulders, ankles, and hands were detected. This can be extended to all human parts. The regression we learned could be used for this application. Here is an example of fiducial point detection:

Fiducial points are landmarks on the face with respect to the location of the eyes, nose, and lips. Finding these landmarks are vital for face-based augmented reality applications. There are some more landmarks available in the face and will be covered in detail in Chapter 6, *Similarity Learning*, in the context of face recognition.

Combining regression with the sliding window

The classification score is computed for every window in the sliding window approach or the fully convolutional approach to know what object is present in that window. Instead of predicting the classification score for every window to detect an object, each window itself can be predicted with a classification score. Combining all the ideas such as sliding window, scale-space, full convolution, and regression give superior results than any individual approach. The following are the top five localization error rates on the ImageNet dataset achieved by various networks using the regression approach:

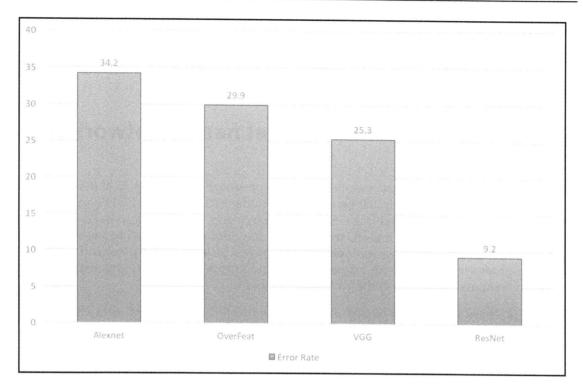

The preceding graph shows that the deeper the network, the better the results. For AlexNet, localization methods were not described in the paper. The OverFeat used multi-scale convolutional regression with box merging. VGG used localization but with fewer scales and location. These gains are attributed to deep features. The ResNet uses a different localization method and much deeper features.

 The regression encoder and classification encoder function independently. Hence there is a possibility of predicting an incorrect label for a bounding box. This problem can be overcome by attaching the regression encoder at different layers. This method could also be used for multiple objects hence solving the object detection problem. Given an image, find all instances in that. It's hard to treat detection as regression because the number of outputs are variable. One image may have two objects and another may have three or more. In the next section, we will see the algorithms dealing with detection problems more effectively.

Detecting objects

There are several variants of object detection algorithms. A few algorithms that come with the object detection API are discussed here.

Regions of the convolutional neural network (R-CNN)

The first work in this series was regions for CNNs proposed by Girshick et al.(`https://arxiv.org/pdf/1311.2524.pdf`). It proposes a few boxes and checks whether any of the boxes correspond to the ground truth. **Selective search** was used for these region proposals. Selective search proposes the regions by grouping the color/texture of windows of various sizes. The selective search looks for blob-like structures. It starts with a pixel and produces a blob at a higher scale. It produces around 2,000 region proposals. This region proposal is less when compared to all the sliding windows possible.

The proposals are resized and passed through a standard CNN architecture such as Alexnet/VGG/Inception/ResNet. The last layer of the CNN is trained with an SVM identifying the object with a no-object class. The boxes are further improved by tightening the boxes around the images. A linear regression model to predict a closer bounding box is trained with object region proposals. The architecture of R-CNN is shown here:

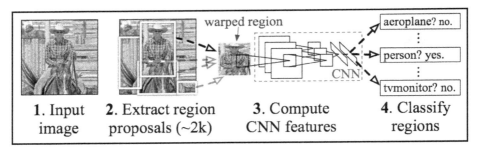

Reproduced with permission from Girshick et al.

The encoder can be a pre-trained model of a standard deep learning model. The features are computed for all the regions from the training data. The features are stored and then the SVM is trained. Next, the bounding boxes are trained with the normalized coordinates. There may be some proposals outside the image coordinates and hence it is normalized for training and inference.

The disadvantages of this method are:

- Several proposals are formed by selective search and hence many inferences have to be computed, usually around 2,000
- There are three classifiers that have to be trained, which increases the number of parameters
- There is no end-to-end training

Fast R-CNN

The Fast R-CNN proposed by Girshick et al. (https://arxiv.org/pdf/1504.08083. pdf)method runs CNN inference only once and hence reduces computations. The output of the CNN is used to propose the networks and select the bounding box. It introduced a technique called **Region of Interest pooling**. The Region of Interest pooling takes the CNN features and pools them together according to the regions. The features obtained after the inference using CNN is pooled and regions are selected, as shown in the following image:

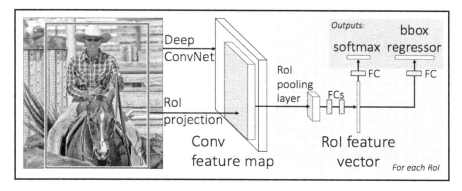

Reproduced with permission from Girshick et al.

This way, an end-to-end training is performed, avoiding multiple classifiers. Note that the SVM is replaced by the softmax layer and the box regressor is replaced by bounding box regressors. The disadvantage that still remains is the selective search, which takes some time.

Faster R-CNN

Faster R-CNN is proposed by Ren et al. (`https://arxiv.org/pdf/1506.01497.pdf`). The difference between Faster R-CNN and the Fast R-CNN method is that the Faster R-CNN uses CNN features of architecture such as VGG and Inception for proposals instead of selective search. The CNN features are further passed through the region proposal network. A sliding window is passed through features with potential bounding boxes and scores as the output, as well as a few aspect ratios that are intuitive, the model outputs bounding box and score:

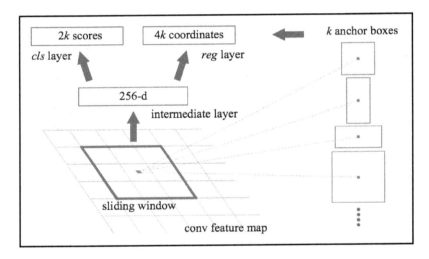

Reproduced with permission from Ren et al.

Faster R-CNN is faster than Fast R-CNN as it saves computation by computing the feature only once.

Single shot multi-box detector

SSD (Single shot multi-box) is proposed by is the fastest of all the methods. This method simultaneously predicts the object and finds the bounding box. During training, there might be a lot of negatives and hence hard-negative mining the class imbalance. The output from CNN has various sizes of features. These are passed to a 3x3 convolutional filter to predict bounding box.

This step predicts the object and bounding box:

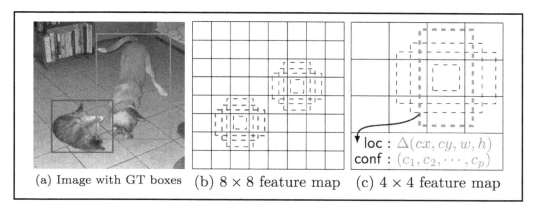

(a) Image with GT boxes (b) 8×8 feature map (c) 4×4 feature map

Reproduced with permission from Liu et al.

These are the algorithms available for object detection and we will learn how to implement them in the following section.

Object detection API

Google released pre-trained models with various algorithms trained on the COCO dataset for public use. The API is built on top of TensorFlow and intended for constructing, training, and deploying object detection models. The APIs support both object detection and localization tasks. The availability of pre-trained models enables the fine-tuning of new data and hence making the training faster. These different models have trade-offs between speed and accuracy.

Installation and setup

Install the Protocol Buffers **(protobuf)** compiler with the following commands. Create a directory for protobuf and download the library directly:

```
mkdir protoc_3.3
cd protoc_3.3
wget https://github.com/google/protobuf/releases/download/v3.3.0/protoc-3.3.0-linux-x86_64.zip
```

Change the permission of the folder and extract the contents, as shown here:

```
chmod 775 protoc-3.3.0-linux-x86_64.zip
unzip protoc-3.3.0-linux-x86_64.zip
```

Protocol Buffers (protobuf) is Google's language-neutral, platform-neutral, extensible mechanism for serializing structured data. It serves the use of XML but is much simpler and faster. The models are usually exported to this format in TensorFlow. One can define the data structure once but can be read or written in a variety of languages. Then run the following command to compile the protobufs. Move back to the working folder and clone the repo from `https://github.com/tensorflow/models.git` and move them to the following folder:

```
git clone https://github.com/tensorflow/models.git
```

Now, move the model to the research folder, using the following code:

```
cd models/research/
~/protoc_3.3/bin/protoc object_detection/protos/*.proto --python_out=.
```

The TensorFlow object detection API uses protobufs for exporting model weights and the training parameters. The TensorFlow, models, research, and slim directories should be appended to PYTHONPATH by the following command:

```
export PYTHONPATH=.:./slim/
```

Adding to the python path with the preceding command works only one time. For the next, this command has to be run again. The installation can be tested by running the following code:

```
python object_detection/builders/model_builder_test.py
```

The output of this code is given here:

```
Ran 7 tests in 0.022s

OK
```

 More information about the installation can be obtained from `https://github.com/tensorflow/models/blob/master/research/object_detection/g3doc/installation.md`. Now the installation is complete and tested.

Pre-trained models

There are several models that are pre-trained and made available. All these models are trained on the COCO dataset and can be used for detecting the objects that are available in the COCO dataset such as humans and cars. These models are also useful for transfer learning for a new task such as traffic sign detection. A table of pre-trained models is shown here with relative speed and mAP on the COCO dataset. Various algorithms are trained with different CNN and are depicted in the names:

Model name	Speed	COCO mAP
ssd_mobilenet_v1_coco	fast	21
ssd_inception_v2_coco	fast	24
rfcn_resnet101_coco	medium	30
faster_rcnn_resnet101_coco	medium	32
faster_rcnn_inception_resnet_v2_atrous_coco	slow	37

Based on the requirement, you can choose from the model. Download the SSD model trained on Mobilenet and extract it as shown here by going to the working directory:

```
mkdir Chapter04 && cd Chapter04
wget
http://download.tensorflow.org/models/object_detection/ssd_mobilenet_v1_coc
o_11_06_2017.tar.gz
tar -xzvf ssd_mobilenet_v1_coco_11_06_2017.tar.gz
```

There will be various files in the Chapter04 folder, which are listed here:

- The is the proto-definition of the graph—graph.pbtxt
- The weights of the graph frozen and can be used for inference—frozen_inference_graph.pb
- Checkpoint files
    - model.ckpt.data-00000-of-00001
    - model.ckpt.meta
    - model.ckpt.index

This model will be used in the next section for detection tasks.

Re-training object detection models

The same API lets us retrain a model for our custom dataset. Training of custom data involves the preparation of a dataset, selecting the algorithm, and performing fine-tuning. The whole pipeline can be passed as a parameter to the training script. The training data has to be converted to TensorFlow records. TensorFlow records is a file format provided by Google to make the reading of data faster than regular files. Now, we will go through the steps of training.

Data preparation for the Pet dataset

The Oxford-IIIT `Pet` dataset is used for this example. Download the image and annotations with these commands from the `Chapter04` directory.

```
wget http://www.robots.ox.ac.uk/~vgg/data/pets/data/images.tar.gz
wget http://www.robots.ox.ac.uk/~vgg/data/pets/data/annotations.tar.gz
```

Extract the image and annotations as shown here:

```
tar -xvf images.tar.gz
tar -xvf annotations.tar.gz
```

Create the `pet_tf` record file to create the dataset in the `tf` records, as they are the required input for the object detection trainer. The `label_map` for the `Pet` dataset can be found at `object_detection/data/pet_label_map.pbtxt`. Move to the `research` folder and run the following command:

```
python object_detection/create_pet_tf_record.py \
    --label_map_path=object_detection/data/pet_label_map.pbtxt \
    --data_dir=~/chapter4/. \
    --output_dir=~/chapter4/.
```

You can see two `.record` files in the research directory named `pet_train.record` and `pet_val.record`.

Object detection training pipeline

The training protobuf has to be configured for training. The following five things are important in this process:

- The model configuration with the type of model
- The `train_config` for standard training parameters

- The `eval_config` for the metrics that have to be reported
- The `train_input_` config for the dataset
- The `eval_input_` config for the evaluation dataset

We will use the config file from `https://github.com/tensorflow/models/blob/master/research/object_detection/samples/configs/ssd_mobilenet_v1_pets.config`. Download it to the `Chapter04` folder by running the following command. Open the `config` file and edit the following lines:

```
fine_tune_checkpoint:
"~/Chapter04/ssd_mobilenet_v1_coco_11_06_2017/model.ckpt"

train_input_reader: {
  tf_record_input_reader {
    input_path: "~/Chapter04/pet_train.record"
  }
  label_map_path:
"~/model/research/object_detection/data/pet_label_map.pbtxt"
}

eval_input_reader: {
  tf_record_input_reader {
    input_path: "~/Chapter04/pet_val.record"
  }
  label_map_path:
"~/model/research/object_detection/data/pet_label_map.pbtxt"
}
```

Save the `config` file. There are various parameters in the file that affect the accuracy of the model.

Training the model

Now the API, data and config files are ready for re-training. The training can be triggered by the following command:

```
PYTHONPATH=.:./slim/. python object_detection/train.py \
    --logtostderr \
    --pipeline_config_path=~/chapter4/ssd_mobilenet_v1_pets.config \
    --train_dir=~/Chapter04
```

The training will start with a loss of around 140 and will keep decreasing. The training will run forever and has to be killed manually by using the *Ctrl* + *C* command. The checkpoints created during the training can be used for inference later.

Monitoring loss and accuracy using TensorBoard

The training loss and accuracy can be monitored using TensorBoard. Run the TensorBoard using the following command:

```
tensorboard --logdir=/home/ubuntu/Chapter04
```

Both training and evaluation can be visualized in the TensorBoard.

Training a pedestrian detection for a self-driving car

The dataset for training a pedestrian object detection can be found at `http://pascal.inrialpes.fr/data/human/`. The steps to detecting pedestrians can be found at `https://github.com/diegocavalca/machine-learning/blob/master/supervisioned/object.detection_tensorflow/simple.detection.ipynb`. The dataset for training a Sign Detector can be downloaded from `http://www.vision.ee.ethz.ch/~timofter/traffic_signs/` and `http://btsd.ethz.ch/shareddata/`. In the case of a self-driving car, there would be four classes in an image for labeling: pedestrian, car, motorcycle, and background. The background class has to be detected when none of the classes is present. An assumption in training a deep learning classification model is that at least one of the objects will be present in the image. By adding the `background` class, we are overcoming the problem. The neural network can also produce a bounding box of the object from the label.

The YOLO object detection algorithm

A recent algorithm for object detection is **You look only once** (**YOLO**). The image is divided into multiple grids. Each grid cell of the image runs the same algorithm. Let's start the implementation by defining layers with initializers:

```
def pooling_layer(input_layer, pool_size=[2, 2], strides=2,
padding='valid'):
    layer = tf.layers.max_pooling2d(
        inputs=input_layer,
        pool_size=pool_size,
        strides=strides,
        padding=padding
    )
    add_variable_summary(layer, 'pooling')
    return layer
```

```
def convolution_layer(input_layer, filters, kernel_size=[3, 3],
padding='valid',
                        activation=tf.nn.leaky_relu):
    layer = tf.layers.conv2d(
        inputs=input_layer,
        filters=filters,
        kernel_size=kernel_size,
        activation=activation,
        padding=padding,
        weights_initializer=tf.truncated_normal_initializer(0.0, 0.01),
        weights_regularizer=tf.l2_regularizer(0.0005)
    )
    add_variable_summary(layer, 'convolution')
    return layer

def dense_layer(input_layer, units, activation=tf.nn.leaky_relu):
    layer = tf.layers.dense(
        inputs=input_layer,
        units=units,
        activation=activation,
        weights_initializer=tf.truncated_normal_initializer(0.0, 0.01),
        weights_regularizer=tf.l2_regularizer(0.0005)
    )
    add_variable_summary(layer, 'dense')
    return layer
```

It can be noticed that the activation layer is `leaky_relu` and the weights are initialized with truncated normal distribution. These modified layers can be used for building the model. The model is created as follows:

```
yolo = tf.pad(images, np.array([[0, 0], [3, 3], [3, 3], [0, 0]]),
name='pad_1')
yolo = convolution_layer(yolo, 64, 7, 2)
yolo = pooling_layer(yolo, [2, 2], 2, 'same')
yolo = convolution_layer(yolo, 192, 3)
yolo = pooling_layer(yolo, 2, 'same')
yolo = convolution_layer(yolo, 128, 1)
yolo = convolution_layer(yolo, 256, 3)
yolo = convolution_layer(yolo, 256, 1)
yolo = convolution_layer(yolo, 512, 3)
yolo = pooling_layer(yolo, 2, 'same')
yolo = convolution_layer(yolo, 256, 1)
yolo = convolution_layer(yolo, 512, 3)
yolo = convolution_layer(yolo, 256, 1)
yolo = convolution_layer(yolo, 512, 3)
yolo = convolution_layer(yolo, 256, 1)
yolo = convolution_layer(yolo, 512, 3)
```

```
yolo = convolution_layer(yolo, 256, 1)
yolo = convolution_layer(yolo, 512, 3)
yolo = convolution_layer(yolo, 512, 1)
yolo = convolution_layer(yolo, 1024, 3)
yolo = pooling_layer(yolo, 2)
yolo = convolution_layer(yolo, 512, 1)
yolo = convolution_layer(yolo, 1024, 3)
yolo = convolution_layer(yolo, 512, 1)
yolo = convolution_layer(yolo, 1024, 3)
yolo = convolution_layer(yolo, 1024, 3)
yolo = tf.pad(yolo, np.array([[0, 0], [1, 1], [1, 1], [0, 0]]))
yolo = convolution_layer(yolo, 1024, 3, 2)
yolo = convolution_layer(yolo, 1024, 3)
yolo = convolution_layer(yolo, 1024, 3)
yolo = tf.transpose(yolo, [0, 3, 1, 2])
yolo = tf.layers.flatten(yolo)
yolo = dense_layer(yolo, 512)
yolo = dense_layer(yolo, 4096)

dropout_bool = tf.placeholder(tf.bool)
yolo = tf.layers.dropout(
        inputs=yolo,
        rate=0.4,
        training=dropout_bool
    )
yolo = dense_layer(yolo, output_size, None)
```

Several convolution layers are stacked, producing the YOLO network. This network is utilized for creating the object detection algorithm for real-time detection.

Summary

In this chapter, we have learned the difference between object localization and detection tasks. Several datasets and evaluation criteria were discussed. Various approaches to localization problems and algorithms, such as variants of R-CNN and SSD models for detection, were discussed. The implementation of detection in open-source repositories was covered. We trained a model for pedestrian detection using the techniques. We also learned about various trade-offs in training such models.

In the next chapter, we will learn about semantic segmentation algorithms. We will use the knowledge to implement the segmentation algorithms for medical imaging and satellite imagery problems.

5
Semantic Segmentation

In this chapter, we will learn about various semantic segmentation techniques and train models for the same. Segmentation is a pixel-wise classification task. The ideas to solve segmentation problem is an extension to object detection problems. Segmentation is highly useful in applications such medical and satellite image understanding.

The following topics will be covered in the chapter:

- Learning the difference between semantic segmentation and instance segmentation
- Segmentation datasets and metrics
- Algorithms for semantic segmentation
- Application of segmentation to medical and satellite images
- Algorithms for instance segmentation

Predicting pixels

Image classification is the task of predicting labels or categories. Object detection is the task of predicting a list of several deep learning-based algorithms with its corresponding bounding box. The bounding box may have objects other than the detected object inside it. In some applications, labeling every pixel to a label is important rather than bounding box which may have multiple objects. **Semantic segmentation** is the task of predicting pixel-wise labels.

Here is an example of an image and its corresponding semantic segmentation:

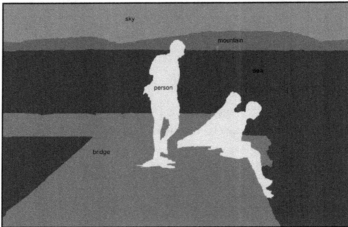

As shown in the image, an input image is predicted with labels for every pixel. The labels could be the sky, tree, person, mountain, and bridge. Rather than assigning a label to the whole image, labels are assigned to each pixel. Semantic segmentation labels pixels independently. You will notice that every people is not distinguished. All the persons in the image are labeled in the same way.

Here is an example where every instance of the same label is distinguished:

This task of segmenting every instance with a pixel-wise label is called **instance segmentation**. Instance segmentation can be thought of as an extension of object detection with pixel-level labels. The applications of semantic segmentation and instance segmentation are enormous, and a few of the applications are provided in the next sections.

Diagnosing medical images

A medical image can be diagnosed with segmentation techniques. Modern medical imaging techniques such as **Magnetic Resonance Imaging (MRI)**, **Computed Tomography (CT)**, and **Retinopathy** create high-quality images. The images generated by such techniques can be segmented into various regions to detect tumours from brain scans or spots from retina scans. Some devices provide volumetric images which can also be analyzed by segmentation. Segmenting the video for robot surgery enables the doctors to see the regions carefully in robot-assisted surgeries. We will see how to segment medical images later in the chapter.

Understanding the earth from satellite imagery

Satellite images have become abundant recently. The images captured by satellite provide a high-resolution view of the total surface of the earth. By analyzing the satellite imagery, we can understand several things about earth such as:

- Measuring the rate of construction in a country related to economic growth
- Measuring the oil tanks
- Planning and organizing the traffic
- Calculating the deforestation and its effects
- Helping wildlife preservation by counting animals and tracking their movements
- Discovering archaeological sites
- Mapping the damaged regions due to a natural disaster

There are more applications possible with satellite imagery. For most of these problems mentioned, the solution starts with the segmentation of satellite images. We will see how to segment satellite images later in the chapter.

Enabling robots to see

Segmenting the scenes is crucial for robots to see and interact with the world around. Industrial and home robots have to handle the objects. The handling becomes possible once the vision to the robots is stridden according to the objects. There are a few more applications worth mentioning:

- Industrial inspection of tools for segmenting the defects
- Color diagnostics of the fashion industry; an image can be segmented with various fashion objects and use them for color parsing
- Distinguish foreground from background to apply portrait effects

In the next section, we will learn a few public datasets for evaluating segmentation algorithms.

Datasets

The PASCAL and COCO datasets that were mentioned in Chapter 4, *Object Detection*, can be used for the segmentation task as well. The annotations are different as they are labelled pixel-wise. New algorithms are usually benchmarked against the COCO dataset. COCO also has stuff datasets such as grass, wall, and sky. The pixel accuracy property can be used as a metric for evaluating algorithms.

Apart from those mentioned, there are several other datasets in the areas of medical imaging and satellite imagery. The links to a few of them are provided here for your reference:

- http://www.cs.bu.edu/~betke/BiomedicalImageSegmentation
- https://www.kaggle.com/c/intel-mobileodt-cervical-cancer-screening/data
- https://www.kaggle.com/c/diabetic-retinopathy-detection
- https://grand-challenge.org/all_challenges
- http://www.via.cornell.edu/databases
- https://www.kaggle.com/c/dstl-satellite-imagery-feature-detection
- https://aws.amazon.com/public-datasets/spacenet
- https://www.iarpa.gov/challenges/fmow.html
- https://www.kaggle.com/c/planet-understanding-the-amazon-from-space

Creating training data for segmentation tasks is expensive. There are online tools available for annotating your dataset. The **LabelMe** mobile application provided by **MIT University** is good for annotating and can be downloaded from http://labelme.csail.mit.edu/Release3.0.

Algorithms for semantic segmentation

There are several deep learning-based algorithms that were proposed to solve image segmentation tasks. A sliding window approach can be applied at a pixel level for segmentation. A sliding window approach takes an image and breaks the image into smaller crops. Every crop of the image is classified for a label. This approach is expensive and inefficient because it doesn't reuse the shared features between the overlapping patches. In the following sections, we will discuss a few algorithms that can overcome this problem.

The Fully Convolutional Network

The **Fully Convolutional Network (FCN)** introduced the idea of an end-to-end convolutional network. Any standard CNN architecture can be used for FCN by removing the fully connected layers, and the implementation of the same was shown in Chapter 4, *Object Detection*. The fully connected layers are replaced by a convolution layer. The depth is higher in the final layers and the size is smaller. Hence, 1D convolution can be performed to reach the desired number of labels. But for segmentation, the spatial dimension has to be preserved. Hence, the full convolution network is constructed without a max pooling, as shown here:

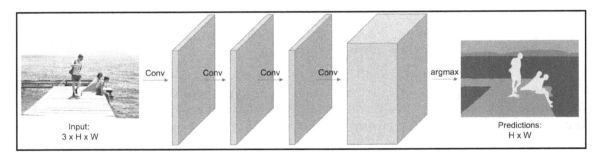

The loss for this network is computed by averaging the cross-entropy loss of every pixel and mini-batch. The final layer has a depth equal to the number of classes. FCN is similar to object detection except that the spatial dimension is preserved. The output produced by the architecture will be coarse as some pixels may be mispredicted. The computation is high and in the next section, we will see how to address this issue.

The SegNet architecture

The **SegNet** has an encoder and decoder approach. The encode has various convolution layers and decoder has various deconvolution layers. SegNet improved the coarse outputs produced by FCN. Because of this, it is less intensive on memory. When the features are reduced in dimensions, it is upsampled again to the image size by deconvolution, reversing the convolution effects. Deconvolution learns the parameters for upsampling. The output of such architecture will be coarse due to the loss of information in pooling layers.

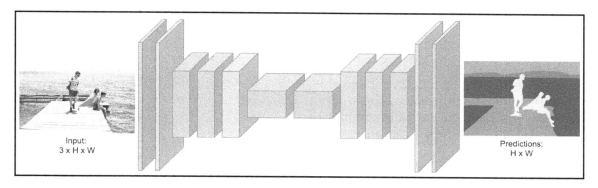

Now, let's learn the few new concepts called upsampling, atrous convolution, and transpose convolution that will help us in understanding this network better.

Upsampling the layers by pooling

In Chapter 1, *Getting Started*, we discussed max pooling. Max pooling is a sampling strategy that picks the maximum value from a window. This could be reversed for upsampling. Each value can be surrounded with zeros to upsample the layer, as shown here:

The zeros are added at the same locations which are the numbers that are upsampled. Unpooling can be improved by remembering the locations of downsampling and using it for upsampling, as shown here:

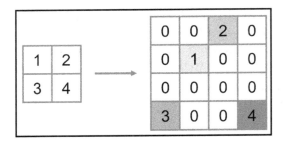

Index-wise, upsampling yields better results than appending zeros. This upsampling the layers by pooling is not learned and works as it is. Next, we will see how we can upsample and downsample with learnable parameters.

Sampling the layers by convolution

The layers can be upsampled or downsampled directly using convolution. The stride used for convolution can be increased to cause downsampling as shown here:

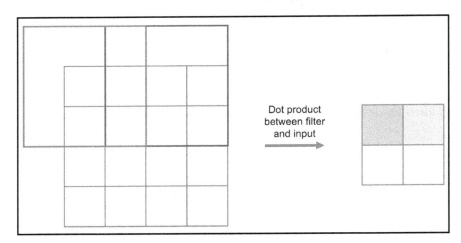

Downsampling by convolution is called **atrous convolution** or **dilated convolution** or **strided convolution**. Similarly, it can be reversed to upsample by learning a kernel as shown here:

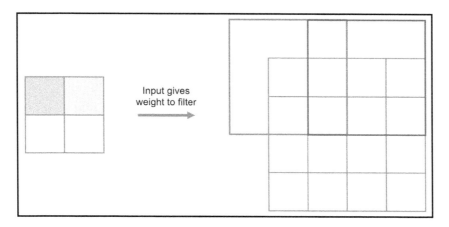

Upsampling directly using a convolution can be termed as **transposed convolution**. Some other synonyms are **deconvolution** or **fractionally strided convolution** or **up-convolution**. Now the process of upsampling is understood. Here is a code snippet that describes the previous algorithm:

```
input_height = 360
input_width = 480
kernel = 3
filter_size = 64
pad = 1
pool_size = 2
```

After the input is taken, it follows the usual convolutional neural net with decreasing size, which can be termed as an encoder. The following code can be used for defining the encoder:

```
model = tf.keras.models.Sequential()
model.add(tf.keras.layers.Layer(input_shape=(3, input_height,
input_width)))

# encoder
model.add(tf.keras.layers.ZeroPadding2D(padding=(pad, pad)))
model.add(tf.keras.layers.Conv2D(filter_size, kernel, kernel,
                      border_mode='valid'))
model.add(tf.keras.layers.BatchNormalization())
model.add(tf.keras.layers.Activation('relu'))
model.add(tf.keras.layers.MaxPooling2D(pool_size=(pool_size, pool_size)))

model.add(tf.keras.layers.ZeroPadding2D(padding=(pad, pad)))
model.add(tf.keras.layers.Conv2D(128, kernel, kernel, border_mode='valid'))
model.add(tf.keras.layers.BatchNormalization())
```

```
model.add(tf.keras.layers.Activation('relu'))
model.add(tf.keras.layers.MaxPooling2D(pool_size=(pool_size, pool_size)))

model.add(tf.keras.layers.ZeroPadding2D(padding=(pad, pad)))
model.add(tf.keras.layers.Conv2D(256, kernel, kernel, border_mode='valid'))
model.add(tf.keras.layers.BatchNormalization())
model.add(tf.keras.layers.Activation('relu'))
model.add(tf.keras.layers.MaxPooling2D(pool_size=(pool_size, pool_size)))

model.add(tf.keras.layers.ZeroPadding2D(padding=(pad, pad)))
model.add(tf.keras.layers.Conv2D(512, kernel, kernel, border_mode='valid'))
model.add(tf.keras.layers.BatchNormalization())
model.add(tf.keras.layers.Activation('relu'))
```

The output of the encoder can be fed to the decoder with increasing size, using the following code:

```
# decoder
model.add(tf.keras.layers.ZeroPadding2D(padding=(pad, pad)))
model.add(tf.keras.layers.Conv2D(512, kernel, kernel, border_mode='valid'))
model.add(tf.keras.layers.BatchNormalization())

model.add(tf.keras.layers.UpSampling2D(size=(pool_size, pool_size)))
model.add(tf.keras.layers.ZeroPadding2D(padding=(pad, pad)))
model.add(tf.keras.layers.Conv2D(256, kernel, kernel, border_mode='valid'))
model.add(tf.keras.layers.BatchNormalization())

model.add(tf.keras.layers.UpSampling2D(size=(pool_size, pool_size)))
model.add(tf.keras.layers.ZeroPadding2D(padding=(pad, pad)))
model.add(tf.keras.layers.Conv2D(128, kernel, kernel, border_mode='valid'))
model.add(tf.keras.layers.BatchNormalization())

model.add(tf.keras.layers.UpSampling2D(size=(pool_size, pool_size)))
model.add(tf.keras.layers.ZeroPadding2D(padding=(pad, pad)))
model.add(tf.keras.layers.Conv2D(filter_size, kernel, kernel,
border_mode='valid'))
model.add(tf.keras.layers.BatchNormalization())

model.add(tf.keras.layers.Conv2D(nClasses, 1, 1, border_mode='valid', ))
```

The decoded image is of the same size as the input, and the whole model can be trained, using the following code:

```
model.outputHeight = model.output_shape[-2]
model.outputWidth = model.output_shape[-1]

model.add(tf.keras.layers.Reshape((nClasses, model.output_shape[-2] *
model.output_shape[-1]),
```

```
                    input_shape=(nClasses, model.output_shape[-2],
model.output_shape[-1])))

model.add(tf.keras.layers.Permute((2, 1)))
model.add(tf.keras.layers.Activation('softmax'))

model.compile(loss="categorical_crossentropy",
optimizer=tf.keras.optimizers.Adam, metrics=['accuracy'])
```

This way of encoding and decoding an image overcomes the shortcomings of FCN-based models. Next, we will see a different concept with dilated convolutions.

Skipping connections for better training

The coarseness of segmentation output can be limited by skip architecture, and higher resolutions can be obtained. Another alternative way is to scale up the last three layers and average them as shown here:

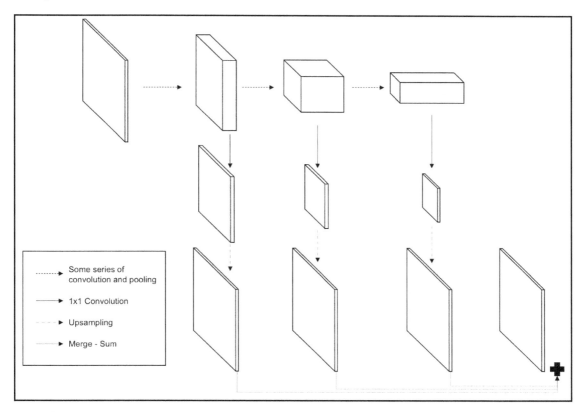

This algorithm is utilized for an example of satellite imagery in a later section.

Dilated convolutions

The pixel-wise classification and image classification are structurally different. Hence, pooling layers that decrease information will produce coarse segmentation. But remember, pooling is essential for having a wider view and allows sampling. A new idea called **dilated convolution** was introduced to solve this problem for less-lossy sampling while having a wider view. The dilated convolution is essentially convolution by skipping every pixel in the window as shown here:

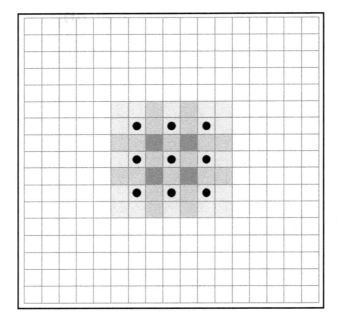

The dilation distance varies from layer to layer. The output of such a segmentation result is upscaled for a finer resolution. A separate network is trained for multi-scale aggregation.

DeepLab

DeepLab proposed by Chen et al. (https://arxiv.org/pdf/1606.00915.pdf) performs convolutions on multiple scales and uses the features from various scales to obtain a score map. The score map is then interpolated and passed through a **conditional random field** (**CRF**) for final segmentation. This scale processing of images can be either performed by processing images of various sizes with its own CNN or parallel convolutions with varying level of dilated convolutions.

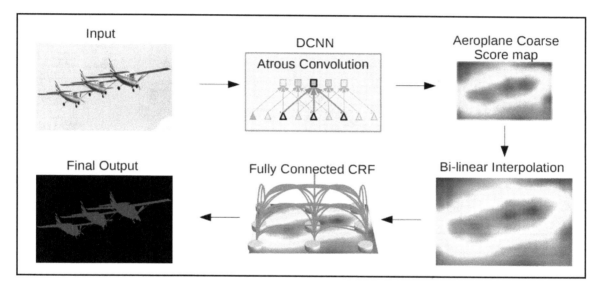

Reproduced with permission from Chen et al.

RefiNet

Dilated convolutions need bigger input and hence, are memory intensive. This presents computational problems when using high-resolution pictures. Reid et al. (`https://arxiv.org/pdf/1611.06612.pdf`) prosed a method called RefiNet to overcome this problem which is shown below:

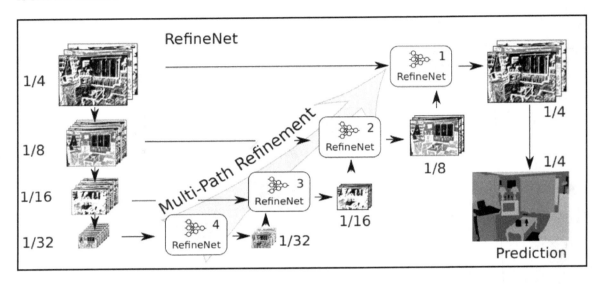

Reproduced with permission from Reid et al.

RefiNet uses an encoder followed by a decoder. Encoder outputs of CNN. The decoder concatenates the features of various sizes:

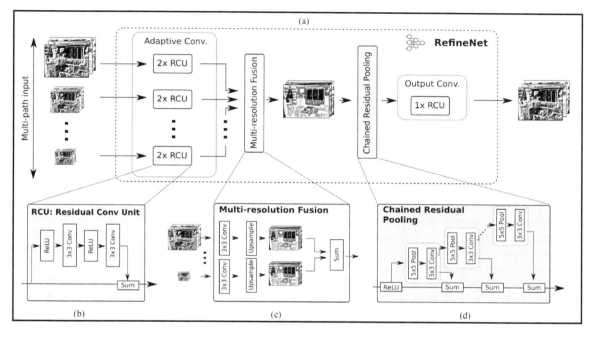

The concatenation is done upscaling the low dimensional feature.

PSPnet

Global content is utilized in PSPnet introduced by Zhoa et al. (https://arxiv.org/pdf/1612.01105.pdf) by increasing the kernel size of pooling layers. The pooling is carried in a pyramid fashion. The pyramid covers various portions and sizes of the images simultaneously. There is a loss in-between the architecture which enables moderate supervision.

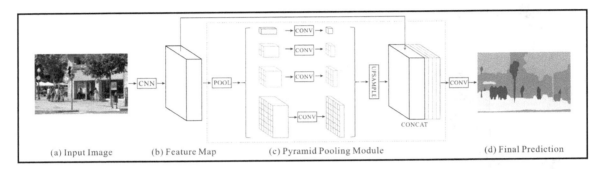

(a) Input Image   (b) Feature Map   (c) Pyramid Pooling Module   (d) Final Prediction

Reproduced with permission from Zhao et al.

Large kernel matters

Peng et al. (https://arxiv.org/pdf/1703.02719.pdf) showcased the importance of large kernels. Large kernels have bigger receptive fields than small kernels. The computational complexity of these large kernels can be used to overcome with an approximate smaller kernel. There is a boundary refinement network at the end.

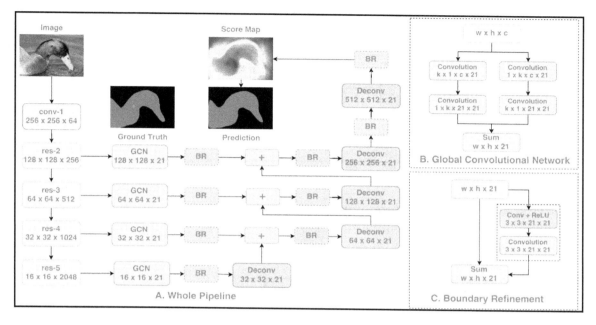

Reproduced with permission from Peng et al.

DeepLab v3

Batch normalization is used in the paper proposed by Chen et al. (https://arxiv.org/pdf/1706.05587.pdf) to improve the performance. The multi-scale of the feature is encoded in a cascaded fashion to improve the performance:

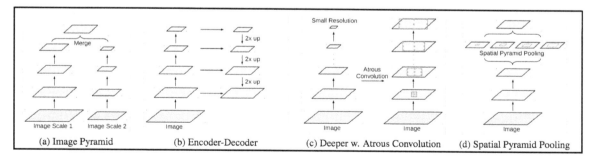

Reproduced with permission from Chen et al.

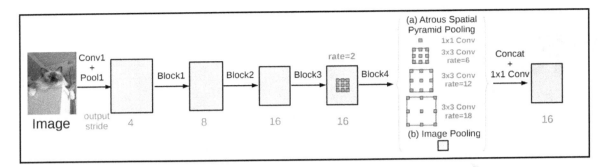

Reproduced with permission from Chen et al.

We have seen several architectures improve the accuracy of image segmentation using deep learning. Next, we will see an application in medical imaging.

Ultra-nerve segmentation

The Kaggler is an organization that conducts competitions on predictive modelling and analytics. The Kagglers were once challenged to segment nerve structures from ultrasound images of the neck. The data regarding the same can be downloaded from `https://www.kaggle.com/c/ultrasound-nerve-segmentation`. The UNET model proposed by Ronneberger et al. (`https://arxiv.org/pdf/1505.04597.pdf`) resembles an autoencoder but with convolutions instead of a fully connected layer. There is an encoding part with the convolution of decreasing dimensions and a decoder part with increasing dimensions as shown here:

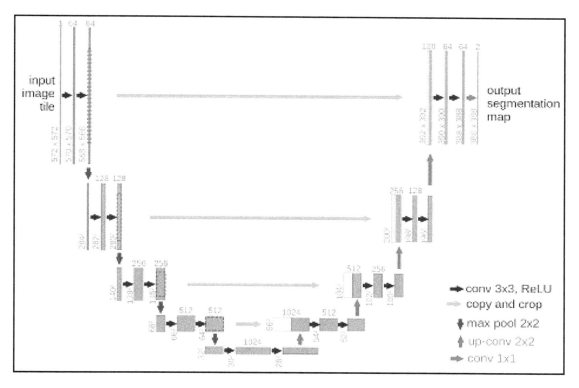

Figure illustrating the architecture of the UNET model [Reproduced with permission from Ronneberger et al.]

The convolutions of the similar sized encoder and decoder part are learning by skip connections. The output of the model is a mask that ranges between 0 and 1. Let's start by importing the functions, with the help of the following code:

```
import os
from skimage.transform import resize
from skimage.io import imsave
import numpy as np
from data import load_train_data, load_test_data
```

After all the imports, we will now define the sizes, using the following code:

```
image_height, image_width = 96, 96
smoothness = 1.0
work_dir = ''
```

Now we will define the `dice_coefficient` and its loss function. The `dice_coefficient` is also the metric in this case:

```
def dice_coefficient(y1, y2):
    y1 = tf.flatten(y1)
    y2 = tf.flatten(y2)
    return (2. * tf.sum(y1 * y2) + smoothness) / (tf.sum(y1) + tf.sum(y2) +
smoothness)


def dice_coefficient_loss(y1, y2):
    return -dice_coefficient(y1, y2)
```

The UNET model can be defined as follows:

```
def preprocess(imgs):
    imgs_p = np.ndarray((imgs.shape[0], image_height, image_width),
dtype=np.uint8)
    for i in range(imgs.shape[0]):
        imgs_p[i] = resize(imgs[i], (image_width, image_height),
preserve_range=True)
    imgs_p = imgs_p[..., np.newaxis]
    return imgs_p


def covolution_layer(filters, kernel=(3,3), activation='relu',
input_shape=None):
    if input_shape is None:
        return tf.keras.layers.Conv2D(
            filters=filters,
            kernel=kernel,
            activation=activation)
    else:
        return tf.keras.layers.Conv2D(
            filters=filters,
            kernel=kernel,
            activation=activation,
            input_shape=input_shape)


def concatenated_de_convolution_layer(filters):
    return tf.keras.layers.concatenate([
        tf.keras.layers.Conv2DTranspose(
            filters=filters,
            kernel=(2, 2),
            strides=(2, 2),
            padding='same'
```

```
        )],
        axis=3
    )
```

All the layers are concatenated and used, as shown in the following code:

```
unet = tf.keras.models.Sequential()
inputs = tf.keras.layers.Input((image_height, image_width, 1))
input_shape = (image_height, image_width, 1)
unet.add(covolution_layer(32, input_shape=input_shape))
unet.add(covolution_layer(32))
unet.add(pooling_layer())

unet.add(covolution_layer(64))
unet.add(covolution_layer(64))
unet.add(pooling_layer())

unet.add(covolution_layer(128))
unet.add(covolution_layer(128))
unet.add(pooling_layer())

unet.add(covolution_layer(256))
unet.add(covolution_layer(256))
unet.add(pooling_layer())

unet.add(covolution_layer(512))
unet.add(covolution_layer(512))
```

The layers are concatenated, and deconvolution layers are used:

```
unet.add(concatenated_de_convolution_layer(256))
unet.add(covolution_layer(256))
unet.add(covolution_layer(256))

unet.add(concatenated_de_convolution_layer(128))
unet.add(covolution_layer(128))
unet.add(covolution_layer(128))

unet.add(concatenated_de_convolution_layer(64))
unet.add(covolution_layer(64))
unet.add(covolution_layer(64))

unet.add(concatenated_de_convolution_layer(32))
unet.add(covolution_layer(32))
unet.add(covolution_layer(32))

unet.add(covolution_layer(1, kernel=(1, 1), activation='sigmoid'))
```

```
unet.compile(optimizer=tf.keras.optimizers.Adam(lr=1e-5),
          loss=dice_coefficient_loss,
          metrics=[dice_coefficient])
```

Next, the model can be trained with images, by making use of the following code:

```
x_train, y_train_mask = load_train_data()

x_train = preprocess(x_train)
y_train_mask = preprocess(y_train_mask)

x_train = x_train.astype('float32')
mean = np.mean(x_train)
std = np.std(x_train)

x_train -= mean
x_train /= std

y_train_mask = y_train_mask.astype('float32')
y_train_mask /= 255.

unet.fit(x_train, y_train_mask, batch_size=32, epochs=20, verbose=1,
shuffle=True,
          validation_split=0.2)

x_test, y_test_mask = load_test_data()
x_test = preprocess(x_test)

x_test = x_test.astype('float32')
x_test -= mean
x_test /= std

y_test_pred = unet.predict(x_test, verbose=1)

for image, image_id in zip(y_test_pred, y_test_mask):
    image = (image[:, :, 0] * 255.).astype(np.uint8)
    imsave(os.path.join(work_dir, str(image_id) + '.png'), image)
```

The image can be pre-processed and used. Now the training and testing of the images can happen. When the model is trained, the segmentation produces good results, as shown here:

We have trained a model that can segment medical images. This algorithm can be used in several use cases. In the next section, we will see how to segment satellite images.

Segmenting satellite images

In this section, we will use a dataset provided by the **International Society for Photogrammetry and Remote Sensing (ISPRS)**. The dataset contains satellite images of Potsdam, Germany with 5 cm resolution. These images come with an additional data of infrared and height contours of the images. There are six labels associated with the images, which are:

- Building
- Vegetation
- Trees
- Cabs
- Clutter
- Impervious

A total of 38 images are provided with 6,000 x 6,000 patches. Please go to the page, `http://www2.isprs.org/commissions/comm3/wg4/data-request-form2.html` and fill in the form. After that, select the following options on the form:

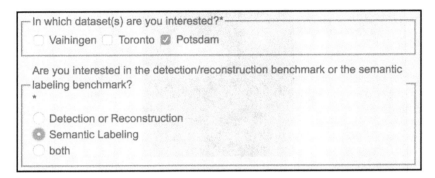

Post the form, an email will be sent to you, from which the data can be downloaded.

Modeling FCN for segmentation

Import the libraries and get the shape of the input. The number of labels is defined as 6:

```
from .resnet50 import ResNet50
nb_labels = 6

img_height, img_width, _ = input_shape
input_tensor = tf.keras.layers.Input(shape=input_shape)
weights = 'imagenet'
```

A `ResNet` model pre-trained on ImageNet will be used as the base model. The following code can be used to define the base model using `ResNet`:

```
resnet50_model = ResNet50(
    include_top=False, weights='imagenet', input_tensor=input_tensor)
```

Now we will use the following code to take the final three layers from the `ResNet`:

```
final_32 = resnet50_model.get_layer('final_32').output
final_16 = resnet50_model.get_layer('final_16').output
final_x8 = resnet50_model.get_layer('final_x8').output
```

Each skip connection has to be compressed to match the channel that is equal to the number of labels:

```
c32 = tf.keras.layers.Conv2D(nb_labels, (1, 1))(final_32)
c16 = tf.keras.layers.Conv2D(nb_labels, (1, 1))(final_16)
c8 = tf.keras.layers.Conv2D(nb_labels, (1, 1))(final_x8)
```

The output of the compressed skip connection can be resized using bilinear interpolation. The interpolation can be implemented by using a `Lambda` layer that can compute TensorFlow operation. The following code snippet can be used for interpolation using the lambda layer:

```
def resize_bilinear(images):
    return tf.image.resize_bilinear(images, [img_height, img_width])


r32 = tf.keras.layers.Lambda(resize_bilinear)(c32)
r16 = tf.keras.layers.Lambda(resize_bilinear)(c16)
r8 = tf.keras.layers.Lambda(resize_bilinear)(c8)
```

The three layers we have defined can be merged by adding the three values, using the following code:

```
m = tf.keras.layers.Add()([r32, r16, r8])
```

The probabilities of the model can be applied using softmax activation. The model is resized before and after applying softmax:

```
x = tf.keras.ayers.Reshape((img_height * img_width, nb_labels))(m)
x = tf.keras.layers.Activation('img_height')(x)
x = tf.keras.layers.Reshape((img_height, img_width, nb_labels))(x)

fcn_model = tf.keras.models.Model(input=input_tensor, output=x)
```

A simple FCN layer has been defined and when trained, it gives the following result:

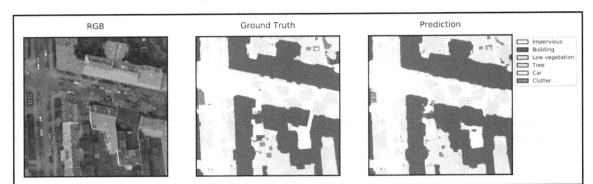

You can see that the prediction of the six labels is reasonable. Next, we will learn about segmenting instances.

Segmenting instances

While analyzing an image, our interest will only be drawn to certain instances in the image. So, it was compelled to segment these instances from the remainder of the image. This process of separating the required information from the rest is widely known as **segmenting instances**. During this process, the input image is first taken, then the bounding box will be localized with the objects and at last, a pixel-wise mask will be predicted for each of the class. For each of the objects, pixel-level accuracy is calculated. There are several algorithms for segmenting instances. One of the recent algorithms is the **Mask RCNN** algorithm proposed by He at al. (https://arxiv.org/pdf/1703.06870.pdf). The following figure portrays the architecture of Mask R-CNN:

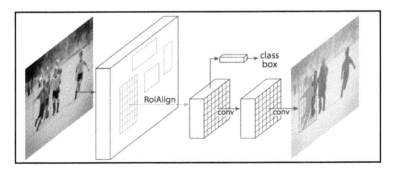

Reproduced with permission from He et al.

The architecture looks similar to the R-CNN with an addition of segmentation. It is a multi-stage network with end-to-end training. The region proposals are learned. The network is split into two, one for detection and the other for a classification score. The results are excellent, as shown here:

Figure illustrating the segmenting instances process, Note that the objects are detected accurately and are segmented accordingly Reproduced with permission from He et al.

The same network can also predict the poses of people. The two tasks of segmentation and detection are processed in parallel.

Summary

In this chapter, we have learned about the various segmentation algorithms. We also saw the datasets and metrics that are used for benchmarking. We applied the techniques learned to segment satellite and medical images. In the end, we touched upon the Mask R-CNN algorithm for instance segmentation.

In the next chapter, we will learn about similarity learning. Similarity learning models learn a comparison mechanism between two images. It is useful for several applications such as face recognition. We will learn several model architectures that can be used for similarity learning.

6
Similarity Learning

In this chapter, we will learn about similarity learning and learn various loss functions used in similarity learning. Similarity learning us useful when the dataset is small per class. We will understand different datasets available for face analysis and build a model for face recognition, landmark detection. We will cover the following topics in this chapter:

- Different algorithms for similarity learning
- Various loss functions used for similarity learning
- A variety of scenarios in which such models can be used
- The complete process of face recognition

Algorithms for similarity learning

Similarity learning is the process of training a metric to compute the similarity between two entities. This could also be termed as metric learning, as the similarity is learned. A metric could be Euclidean or cosine or some other custom distance function. Entities could be any data such as an image, video, text or tables. To compute a metric, a vector representation of the image is required. This representation can be the features computed by a CNN as described in Chapter 3, *Image Retrieval*. The CNN that was learned for object classification can be used as the vector to compute the metric. The feature vector obtained for image classification would not be the best representation of the task at hand. In similarity learning, we find out about CNNs that generate features trained for a similarity learning task. Some applications of similarity learning are given here:

- Face verification for biometrics to compare two faces
- Visual search of real-world objects to find similar products online
- Visual recommendation of products that are similar in some attributes

In this chapter, we will learn about face verification in detail. So let's start with the algorithms that are available for similarity learning.

Siamese networks

A Siamese network, as the name suggests, is a neural network model where the network is trained to distinguish between two inputs. A Siamese network can train a CNN to produced an embedding by two encoders. Each encoder is fed with one of the images in either a positive or a negative pair. A Siamese network requires less data than the other deep learning algorithms. Siamese networks were originally introduced for comparing signatures. A Siamese network is shown in the following image; the weights are shared between the networks:

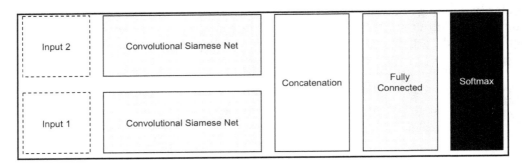

The other use of Siamese networks is one-shot learning. **One-shot learning** is the technique of learning with just one example. In this case, an image can be shown and it can tell whether they are similar. For most of the similarity learning tasks, a pair of positive and negative pairs are required to train. Such datasets can be formed with any dataset that is available for classification tasks, assuming that they are Euclidean distances. The main difference between these algorithms and algorithms in previous chapters is that these encoders try to differentiate one from another.

Contrastive loss

Contrastive loss differentiates images by similarity. The feature or latent layer is compared using a similarity metric and trained with the target for a similarity score. In the case of a positive pair, the target would be 0, as both inputs are the same. For negative pairs, the distance between the pair of latent is a maximum of 0 in the case of cosine distance or regularised Euclidean distance. The loss can be defined by a `contrastive_loss`, which is explained in the following code:

```
def contrastive_loss(model_1, model_2, label, margin=0.1):
    distance = tf.reduce_sum(tf.square(model_1 - model_2), 1)
    loss = label * tf.square(
        tf.maximum(0., margin - tf.sqrt(distance))) + (1 - label) *
distance
    loss = 0.5 * tf.reduce_mean(loss)
    return loss
```

Two model's distances are compared and loss is computed. Now, we will define and train a Siamese network. For a Siamese network, we will need two models that are same. Next, let's define a function for a simple CNN with a given input, with the help of the following code:

```
def get_model(input_):
    input_reshape = tf.reshape(input_, [-1, 28, 28, 1],
                               name='input_reshape')
    convolution_layer_1 = convolution_layer(input_reshape, 64)
    pooling_layer_1 = pooling_layer(convolution_layer_1)
    convolution_layer_2 = convolution_layer(pooling_layer_1, 128)
    pooling_layer_2 = pooling_layer(convolution_layer_2)
    flattened_pool = tf.reshape(pooling_layer_2, [-1, 5 * 5 * 128],
                                name='flattened_pool')
    dense_layer_bottleneck = dense_layer(flattened_pool, 1024)
    return dense_layer_bottleneck
```

The model defined will be used twice to define the encoders necessary for Siamese networks. Next, placeholders for both the models are defined. For every pair, the similarity of the inputs is also fed as input. The models defined are the same. The models can also be defined so that the weights are shared. Two models for the left and right side are defined here:

```
left_input = tf.placeholder(tf.float32, shape=[None, input_size])
right_input = tf.placeholder(tf.float32, shape=[None, input_size])
y_input = tf.placeholder(tf.float32, shape=[None, no_classes])
left_bottleneck = get_model(left_input)
right_bottleneck = get_model(right_input)
```

The bottleneck layers are taken from the models and are concatenated. This is crucial for similarity learning problems. Any number of models can be created, and the final layers can be concatenated, as shown here:

```
dense_layer_bottleneck = tf.concat([left_bottleneck, right_bottleneck], 1)
```

Next, a dropout layer is added with logits computed out of the concatenated layer. Then the procedure is similar to any other network, as shown here:

```
dropout_bool = tf.placeholder(tf.bool)
dropout_layer = tf.layers.dropout(
```

```
        inputs=dense_layer_bottleneck,
        rate=0.4,
        training=dropout_bool
    )
logits = dense_layer(dropout_layer, no_classes)

with tf.name_scope('loss'):
    softmax_cross_entropy = tf.nn.softmax_cross_entropy_with_logits(
        labels=y_input, logits=logits)
    loss_operation = tf.reduce_mean(softmax_cross_entropy, name='loss')
    tf.summary.scalar('loss', loss_operation)

with tf.name_scope('optimiser'):
    optimiser = tf.train.AdamOptimizer().minimize(loss_operation)

with tf.name_scope('accuracy'):
    with tf.name_scope('correct_prediction'):
        predictions = tf.argmax(logits, 1)
        correct_predictions = tf.equal(predictions, tf.argmax(y_input, 1))
    with tf.name_scope('accuracy'):
        accuracy_operation = tf.reduce_mean(
            tf.cast(correct_predictions, tf.float32))
tf.summary.scalar('accuracy', accuracy_operation)

session = tf.Session()
session.run(tf.global_variables_initializer())

merged_summary_operation = tf.summary.merge_all()
train_summary_writer = tf.summary.FileWriter('/tmp/train', session.graph)
test_summary_writer = tf.summary.FileWriter('/tmp/test')

test_images, test_labels = mnist_data.test.images, mnist_data.test.labels
```

The data has to be fed separately for left and right models as shown:

```
for batch_no in range(total_batches):
    mnist_batch = mnist_data.train.next_batch(batch_size)
    train_images, train_labels = mnist_batch[0], mnist_batch[1]
    _, merged_summary = session.run([optimiser, merged_summary_operation],
                                    feed_dict={
        left_input: train_images,
        right_input: train_images,
        y_input: train_labels,
        dropout_bool: True
    })
    train_summary_writer.add_summary(merged_summary, batch_no)
    if batch_no % 10 == 0:
        merged_summary, _ = session.run([merged_summary_operation,
```

```
                                         accuracy_operation], feed_dict={
        left_input: test_images,
        right_input: test_images,
        y_input: test_labels,
        dropout_bool: False
    })
    test_summary_writer.add_summary(merged_summary, batch_no)
```

We have seen how to define a Siamese network. Two encoders are defined, and the latent space is concatenated to form the loss of training. The left and right models are fed with data separately. Next, we will see how similarity learning can be performed within a single network.

FaceNet

The FaceNet model proposed by Schroff et al. (`https://arxiv.org/pdf/1503.03832.pdf`) solves the face verification problem. It learns one deep CNN, then transforms a face image to an embedding. The embedding can be used to compare faces to see how similar they are and can be used in the following three ways:

- **Face verification** considers two faces and it is decides whether they are similar or not. Face verification can be done by computing the distance metric.
- **Face recognition** is a classification problem for labelling a face with a name. The embedding vector can be used for training the final labels.
- **Face Clustering** groups similar faces together like how photo applications cluster photos of the same person together. A clustering algorithm such as K-means is used to group faces.

The following image shows the FaceNet architecture:

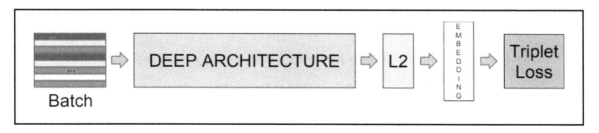

Reproduced with permission from Schroff et al.

FaceNet takes a batch of face images and trains them. In that batch, there will be a few positive pairs. While computing the loss, the positive pairs and closest few negative pairs are considered. Mining selective pairs enable smooth training. If all the negatives are pushed away all the time, the training is not stable. Comparing three data points is called **triplet loss**. The images are considered with a positive and negative match while computing the loss. The negatives are pushed only by a certain margin. Triplet loss is explained in detail here.

Triplet loss

The triplet loss learns the score vectors for the images. The score vectors of face descriptors can be used to verify the faces in Euclidean space. The triplet loss is similar to metric learning in the sense of learning a projection so that the inputs can be distinguished. These projections or descriptors or score vectors are a compact representation, hence can be considered as a dimensionality reduction technique. A triplet consists of an anchor, and positive and negative faces. An anchor can be any face, and positive faces are the images of the same person. The negative image may come from another person. It's obvious that there will be a lot of negative faces for a given anchor. By selecting negatives that are currently closer to the anchor, its harder for the encoder to distinguish the faces, thereby making it learn better. This process is termed as **hard negative mining**. The closer negatives can be obtained with a threshold in Euclidean space. The following image depicts the triplet loss model:

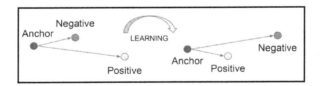

Reproduced with permission from Schroff et al.

The loss computation in TensorFlow is shown here:

```
def triplet_loss(anchor_face, positive_face, negative_face, margin):
    def get_distance(x, y):
        return tf.reduce_sum(tf.square(tf.subtract(x, y)), 1)

    positive_distance = get_distance(anchor_face, positive_face)
    negative_distance = get_distance(anchor_face, negative_face)
    total_distance = tf.add(tf.subtract(positive_distance,
negative_distance), margin)
    return tf.reduce_mean(tf.maximum(total_distance, 0.0), 0)
```

The mining of the triplets is a difficult task. Every point has to be compared with others to get the proper anchor and positive pairs. The mining of the triplets is shown here:

```
def mine_triplets(anchor, targets, negative_samples):
    distances = cdist(anchor, targets, 'cosine')
    distances = cdist(anchor, targets, 'cosine').tolist()
    QnQ_duplicated = [
        [target_index for target_index, dist in enumerate(QnQ_dist) if dist
== QnQ_dist[query_index]]
        for query_index, QnQ_dist in enumerate(distances)]
    for i, QnT_dist in enumerate(QnT_dists):
        for j in QnQ_duplicated[i]:
            QnT_dist.itemset(j, np.inf)

    QnT_dists_topk = QnT_dists.argsort(axis=1)[:, :negative_samples]
    top_k_index = np.array([np.insert(QnT_dist, 0, i) for i, QnT_dist in
enumerate(QnT_dists_topk)])
    return top_k_index
```

This could make the training slower on a GPU machine as the distance computation happens in CPU. The FaceNet model is a state of the art method in training similarity models for faces.

The DeepNet model

The DeepNet model is used for learning the embedding of faces for face verification tasks such as FaceNet. This improves on the method of FaceNet discussed in the previous section. It takes multiple crops of the same face and passes through several encoders to get a better embedding. This has achieved a better accuracy than FaceNet but takes more time for processing. The face crops are made in the same regions and passed through its respective encoders. Then all the layers are concatenated for training against the triplet loss.

DeepRank

DeepRank proposed by Wang et al. (https://users.eecs.northwestern.edu/~jwa368/pdfs/deep_ranking.pdf) is used to rank images based on similarity. Images are passed through different models as shown here:

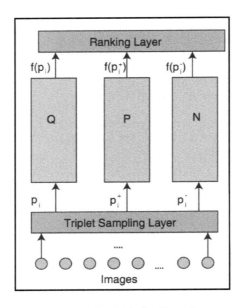

Reproduced with permission from Wang et al.

The triplet loss is computed here as well and backpropagation is done more smoothly. Then the image can be converted to a linear embedding for ranking purposes, as shown:

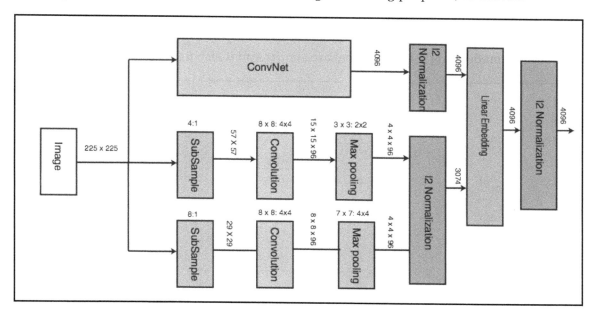

Reproduced with permission from Wang et al.

This algorithm is highly useful for ranking purposes.

Visual recommendation systems

Visual recommendation systems are excellent for getting recommendations for a given image. Recommendation models provide images with similar properties. From the following model proposed by Shankar et al. (`https://arxiv.org/pdf/1703.02344.pdf`) you can learn the embedding for images that are similar and it also provides recommendations:

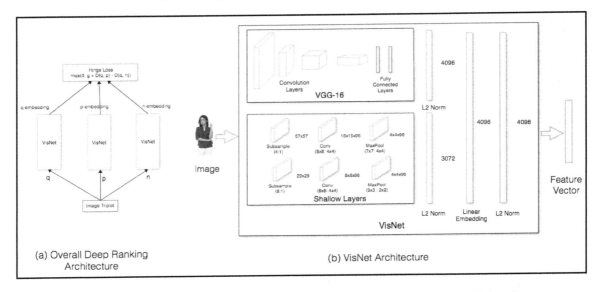

Figure (a) Shows the deep ranking architecture and (b) Shows the VisNet architecture [Reproduced with permission from Shankar et al]

These are some of the algorithms that are used for similarity learning. In the next section, we will see how to apply these techniques to faces.

Human face analysis

The human face can be analyzed in multiple ways using computer vision. There are several factors that are to be considered for this, which are listed here:

- **Face detection**: Finding the bounding box of location of faces
- **Facial landmark detection**: Finding the spatial points of facial features such as nose, mouth and so on

- **Face alignment**: Transforming the face into a frontal face for further analysis
- **Attribute recognition**: Finding attributes such as gender, smiling and so on
- **Emotion analysis**: Analysing the emotions of persons
- **Face verification**: Finding whether two images belong to the same person
- **Face recognition**: Finding an identity for the face
- **Face clustering**: Grouping the faces of the same person together

Let's learn about the datasets and implementation of these tasks in detail, in the following sections.

Face detection

Face detection is similar to the object detection, that we discussed in `Chapter 4`, *Object Detection*. The locations of the faces have to be detected from the image. A dataset called **Face Detection Data Set and Benchmark** (**FDDB**) can be downloaded from `http://vis-www.cs.umass.edu/fddb/`. It has 2,845 images with 5,171 faces. Another dataset called **wider face** can be downloaded from `http://mmlab.ie.cuhk.edu.hk/projects/WIDERFace/` proposed by Yang et al. It has 32,203 images with 393,703 faces. Here is a sample of images from the wider face dataset:

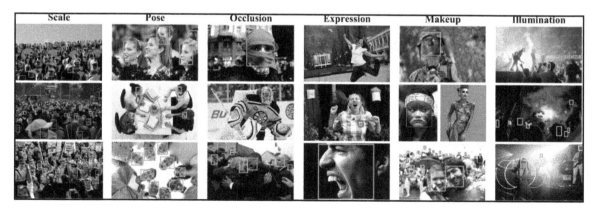

Proposed by Yang et al. and reproduced from http://mmlab.ie.cuhk.edu.hk/projects/WIDERFace/support/intro.jpg

The dataset has a good variation of scale, pose, occlusion, expression, makeup, and illumination. Another dataset called **Multi-Attribute Labelled Faces** (**MALF**) has 5,250 images with 11,931 faces. MALF can be accessed from the link `http://www.cbsr.ia.ac.cn/faceevaluation/`. The same techniques used in object detection can be applied for face detection as well.

Face landmarks and attributes

Face landmarks are the spatial points in a human face. The spatial points correspond to locations of various facial features such as eyes, eyebrows, nose, mouth, and chin. The number of points may vary from 5 to 78 depending on the annotation. Face landmarks are also referred to as **fiducial-points**, **facial key points**, or **face pose**. The face landmarks have many applications as listed here:

- Alignment of faces for better face verification or face recognition
- To track faces in a video
- Facial expressions or emotions can be measured
- Helpful for diagnosis of medical conditions

Next, we will see some databases that have the annotation for fiducial points.

The Multi-Task Facial Landmark (MTFL) dataset

The `MTFL` dataset is proposed by Zhang et al. and is annotated with five facial landmarks along with gender, smiling, glasses and head pose annotations. There are 12,995 faces present in the database. `MTFL` can be downloaded from `http://mmlab.ie.cuhk.edu.hk/projects/TCDCN/data/MTFL.zip`.

Here is a sample of the images present in `MTFL`:

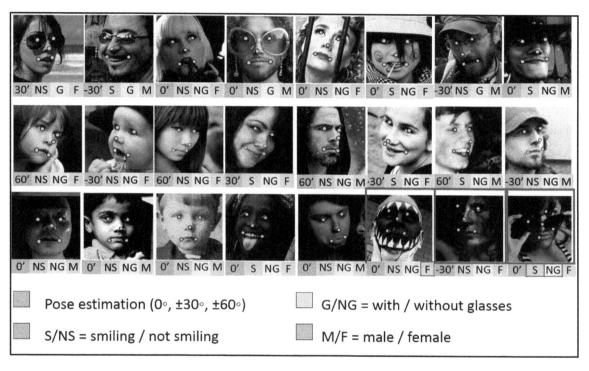

Proposed by Zhang et al. and reproduced from http://mmlab.ie.cuhk.edu.hk/projects/TCDCN/img/1.jpg

There are a lot of variations in the faces with respect to age, illumination, emotions and so on. **Head pose** is the angle of face direction, denoted in degrees. Glasses, smiling, gender attributes, and so on are annotated with binary labels.

The Kaggle keypoint dataset

The Kaggle keypoint dataset is annotated with 15 facial landmarks. There are 8,832 images present in the dataset. It can be downloaded from the link `https://www.kaggle.com/c/facial-keypoints-detection/data`. The images are 96 pixels by 96 pixels in size.

The Multi-Attribute Facial Landmark (MAFL) dataset

The MAFL dataset proposed by Zhang et al. is annotated with 5 facial landmarks with 40 different facial attributes. There are 20,000 faces present in the database. MAFL can be downloaded from `https://github.com/zhzhanp/TCDCN-face-alignment`. Here is a sample of the images present in MAFL:

Proposed by Liu et al. and reproduced from http://mmlab.ie.cuhk.edu.hk/projects/celeba/overview.png

The attributes of annotation include pointy-nose, bands, moustache, wavy hair, wearing a hat and so on. These images are included in the CelebA dataset as well, which will be discussed in detail later.

Learning the facial key points

As discussed in the earlier topics, there are a few parameters that are to be defined while calculating the key facial points. We will use the following code to define these parameters:

```
image_size = 40
no_landmark = 10
no_gender_classes = 2
no_smile_classes = 2
no_glasses_classes = 2
no_headpose_classes = 5
batch_size = 100
total_batches = 300
```

Next, allow a few placeholders for the various inputs.

```
image_input = tf.placeholder(tf.float32, shape=[None, image_size,
image_size])
landmark_input = tf.placeholder(tf.float32, shape=[None, no_landmark])
gender_input = tf.placeholder(tf.float32, shape=[None, no_gender_classes])
smile_input = tf.placeholder(tf.float32, shape=[None, no_smile_classes])
glasses_input = tf.placeholder(tf.float32, shape=[None,
no_glasses_classes])
headpose_input = tf.placeholder(tf.float32, shape=[None,
no_headpose_classes])
```

Next, construct the main model with four convolution layers, as shown in the following code:

```
image_input_reshape = tf.reshape(image_input, [-1, image_size, image_size,
1],
                        name='input_reshape')

convolution_layer_1 = convolution_layer(image_input_reshape, 16)
pooling_layer_1 = pooling_layer(convolution_layer_1)
convolution_layer_2 = convolution_layer(pooling_layer_1, 48)
pooling_layer_2 = pooling_layer(convolution_layer_2)
convolution_layer_3 = convolution_layer(pooling_layer_2, 64)
pooling_layer_3 = pooling_layer(convolution_layer_3)
convolution_layer_4 = convolution_layer(pooling_layer_3, 64)
flattened_pool = tf.reshape(convolution_layer_4, [-1, 5 * 5 * 64],
                        name='flattened_pool')
dense_layer_bottleneck = dense_layer(flattened_pool, 1024)
dropout_bool = tf.placeholder(tf.bool)
dropout_layer = tf.layers.dropout(
        inputs=dense_layer_bottleneck,
        rate=0.4,
```

```
            training=dropout_bool
    )
```

Next, we will create a branch of logits for all the different tasks, by making use of the following code:

```
landmark_logits = dense_layer(dropout_layer, 10)
smile_logits = dense_layer(dropout_layer, 2)
glass_logits = dense_layer(dropout_layer, 2)
gender_logits = dense_layer(dropout_layer, 2)
headpose_logits = dense_layer(dropout_layer, 5)
```

The loss is computed individually for all the facial features, as shown in the following code:

```
landmark_loss = 0.5 * tf.reduce_mean(
    tf.square(landmark_input, landmark_logits))

gender_loss = tf.reduce_mean(
    tf.nn.softmax_cross_entropy_with_logits(
        labels=gender_input, logits=gender_logits))

smile_loss = tf.reduce_mean(
    tf.nn.softmax_cross_entropy_with_logits(
        labels=smile_input, logits=smile_logits))

glass_loss = tf.reduce_mean(
    tf.nn.softmax_cross_entropy_with_logits(
        labels=glasses_input, logits=glass_logits))

headpose_loss = tf.reduce_mean(
    tf.nn.softmax_cross_entropy_with_logits(
        labels=headpose_input, logits=headpose_logits))

loss_operation = landmark_loss + gender_loss + \
                smile_loss + glass_loss + headpose_loss
```

Now, we will initialize the optimizer and start the training, as shown in the following code:

```
optimiser = tf.train.AdamOptimizer().minimize(loss_operation)
session = tf.Session()
session.run(tf.initialize_all_variables())
fiducial_test_data = fiducial_data.test

for batch_no in range(total_batches):
    fiducial_data_batch = fiducial_data.train.next_batch(batch_size)
    loss, _landmark_loss, _ = session.run(
        [loss_operation, landmark_loss, optimiser],
        feed_dict={
```

```
        image_input: fiducial_data_batch.images,
        landmark_input: fiducial_data_batch.landmarks,
        gender_input: fiducial_data_batch.gender,
        smile_input: fiducial_data_batch.smile,
        glasses_input: fiducial_data_batch.glasses,
        headpose_input: fiducial_data_batch.pose,
        dropout_bool: True
    })
if batch_no % 10 == 0:
    loss, _landmark_loss, _ = session.run(
        [loss_operation, landmark_loss],
        feed_dict={
            image_input: fiducial_test_data.images,
            landmark_input: fiducial_test_data.landmarks,
            gender_input: fiducial_test_data.gender,
            smile_input: fiducial_test_data.smile,
            glasses_input: fiducial_test_data.glasses,
            headpose_input: fiducial_test_data.pose,
            dropout_bool: False
        })
```

This process can be used to detect the facial features as well as landmarks.

Face recognition

The **face recognition** or **facial recognition** is the process of identifying a personage from a digital image or a video. Let's learn about the datasets available for face recognition in the next sections.

The labeled faces in the wild (LFW) dataset

The `LFW` dataset contains 13,233 faces with 5,749 unique people and is considered as the standard dataset to evaluate face verification datasets. An accuracy metric can be used to assess the algorithms. The dataset can be accessed in the link `http://vis-www.cs.umass.edu/lfw/`.

The YouTube faces dataset

The YouTube `faces` dataset contains 3,425 video clips with 1,595 unique people. The videos are collected from YouTube. The dataset has at least two videos per person. This dataset is considered as a standard dataset for face verification in videos. The dataset can be accessed in the link `https://www.cs.tau.ac.il/~wolf/ytfaces/`.

The CelebFaces Attributes dataset (CelebA)

The `CelebA` dataset is annotated with identities of people along with 5 facial landmarks and 40 attributes. There are 10,177 unique people with 202,599 face images in the database. It is one of the large datasets available for face verification, detection, landmark and attributes recognition problems. The images have good variations of faces with diverse annotations. The dataset can be accessed in the link `http://mmlab.ie.cuhk.edu.hk/projects/CelebA.html`.

CASIA web face database

The `CASIA` dataset is annotated with 10,575 unique people with 494,414 images in total. The dataset can be obtained from `http://www.cbsr.ia.ac.cn/english/CASIA-WebFace-Database.html`. This is the second largest public dataset available for face verification and recognition problems.

The VGGFace2 dataset

The `VGGFace2` dataset proposed by Cao et al. is annotated with 9,131 unique people with 3.31 million images. The dataset can be obtained from `http://www.robots.ox.ac.uk/~vgg/data/vgg_face2/`. The variation includes age, ethnicity, pose, profession, and illumination. This is the largest dataset available for face verification.

Here is a sample of the images present in the dataset:

Proposed by Cao et al. and reproduced from http://www.robots.ox.ac.uk/~vgg/data/vgg_face2/web_page_img.png

The minimum, mean, and maximum number of images per unique person are 87, 362.6, and 843 respectively.

Computing the similarity between faces

The computing of face similarities is a multi-step problem. The faces have to be detected, followed by finding the fiducial points. The faces can be aligned with the fiducial points. The aligned face can be used for comparison. As I have mentioned earlier, face detection is similar to object detection. So, in order to find the similarities between faces, we will first import the required libraries and also the `facenet` library, with the help of the following code:

```
from scipy import misc
import tensorflow as tf
import numpy as np
import os
import facenet
print facenet
from facenet import load_model, prewhiten
import align.detect_face
```

The images can be loaded and aligned as shown:

```
def load_and_align_data(image_paths, image_size=160, margin=44,
gpu_memory_fraction=1.0):
    minsize = 20
    threshold = [0.6, 0.7, 0.7]
    factor = 0.709

    print('Creating networks and loading parameters')
    with tf.Graph().as_default():
        gpu_options =
tf.GPUOptions(per_process_gpu_memory_fraction=gpu_memory_fraction)
        sess = tf.Session(config=tf.ConfigProto(gpu_options=gpu_options,
log_device_placement=False))
        with sess.as_default():
            pnet, rnet, onet = align.detect_face.create_mtcnn(sess, None)

    nrof_samples = len(image_paths)
    img_list = [None] * nrof_samples
    for i in range(nrof_samples):
        img = misc.imread(os.path.expanduser(image_paths[i]), mode='RGB')
        img_size = np.asarray(img.shape)[0:2]
        bounding_boxes, _ = align.detect_face.detect_face(img, minsize,
pnet, rnet, onet, threshold, factor)
        det = np.squeeze(bounding_boxes[0, 0:4])
        bb = np.zeros(4, dtype=np.int32)
        bb[0] = np.maximum(det[0] - margin / 2, 0)
        bb[1] = np.maximum(det[1] - margin / 2, 0)
        bb[2] = np.minimum(det[2] + margin / 2, img_size[1])
        bb[3] = np.minimum(det[3] + margin / 2, img_size[0])
        cropped = img[bb[1]:bb[3], bb[0]:bb[2], :]
        aligned = misc.imresize(cropped, (image_size, image_size),
interp='bilinear')
        prewhitened = prewhiten(aligned)
        img_list[i] = prewhitened
    images = np.stack(img_list)
    return images
```

Now we will process the image paths to get the embeddings. The code for the same is given here:

```
def get_face_embeddings(image_paths, model='/20170512-110547/'):
    images = load_and_align_data(image_paths)
    with tf.Graph().as_default():
            with tf.Session() as sess:
                    load_model(model)
                    images_placeholder =
tf.get_default_graph().get_tensor_by_name("input:0")
                    embeddings =
tf.get_default_graph().get_tensor_by_name("embeddings:0")
                    phase_train_placeholder =
tf.get_default_graph().get_tensor_by_name("phase_train:0")
                    feed_dict = {images_placeholder: images,
phase_train_placeholder: False}
                    emb = sess.run(embeddings, feed_dict=feed_dict)

    return emb
```

Now we will compute the distance between the embeddings using the following code:

```
def compute_distance(embedding_1, embedding_2):
    dist = np.sqrt(np.sum(np.square(np.subtract(embedding_1,
embedding_2))))
    return dist
```

This function will compute the **Euclidean** distance between the embeddings.

Finding the optimum threshold

Using the preceding functions, the accuracy of this system can be calculated. The following code can be used for calculating the optimum threshold:

```
import sys
import argparse
import os
import re
from sklearn.metrics import classification_report
from sklearn.metrics import accuracy_score
```

Now, the image paths are obtained from the folder, using the following code:

```
def get_image_paths(image_directory):
    image_names = sorted(os.listdir(image_directory))
    image_paths = [os.path.join(image_directory, image_name) for image_name
in image_names]
    return image_paths
```

The distances of the images are obtained when embeddings are passed, as shown in the following code:

```
def get_labels_distances(image_paths, embeddings):
    target_labels, distances = [], []
    for image_path_1, embedding_1 in zip(image_paths, embeddings):
        for image_path_2, embedding_2 in zip(image_paths, embeddings):
            if (re.sub(r'\d+', '', image_path_1)).lower() ==
(re.sub(r'\d+', '', image_path_2)).lower():
                target_labels.append(1)
            else:
                target_labels.append(0)
            distances.append(compute_distance(embedding_1, embedding_2)) #
Replace distance metric here
    return target_labels, distances
```

The threshold is varied as shown in the following code and various metrics are printed accordingly:

```
def print_metrics(target_labels, distances):
    accuracies = []
    for threshold in range(50, 150, 1):
        threshold = threshold/100.
        predicted_labels = [1 if dist <= threshold else 0 for dist in
distances]
        print("Threshold", threshold)
        print(classification_report(target_labels, predicted_labels,
target_names=['Different', 'Same']))
        accuracy = accuracy_score(target_labels, predicted_labels)
        print('Accuracy: ', accuracy)
        accuracies.append(accuracy)
    print(max(accuracies))
```

Now, the image paths are passed to the embeddings, with the help of the following code:

```
def main(args):
    image_paths = get_image_paths(args.image_directory)
    embeddings = get_face_embeddings(image_paths)  # Replace your embedding
calculation here
    target_labels, distances = get_labels_distances(image_paths,
embeddings)
    print_metrics(target_labels, distances)
```

Finally, the directory of the images is passed as the main argument to these methods, as shown in the following code:

```
if __name__ == '__main__':
    parser = argparse.ArgumentParser()
    parser.add_argument('image_directory', type=str, help='Directory
containing the images to be compared')
    parsed_arguments = parser.parse_args(sys.argv[1:])
    main(parsed_arguments)
```

In this example, we have taken a pre-trained model and used it to construct a face verification method. ;

Face clustering

Face clustering is the process of grouping images of the same person together for albums. The embeddings of faces can be extracted, and a clustering algorithm such as K-means can be used to club the faces of the same person together. TensorFlow provides an API called `tf.contrib.learn.KmeansClustering` for the K-means algorithm. The K-means algorithm groups the data points together. With the help of this K-means algorithm, the embeddings of an album can be extracted and the faces of individuals can be found together, or in other words, clustered together.

Summary

In this chapter, we covered the basics of similarity learning. We studied algorithms such as metric learning, Siamese networks, and FaceNet. We also covered loss functions such as contrastive loss and triplet loss. Two different domains, ranking and recommendation, were also covered. Finally, the step-by-step walkthrough of face identification was covered by understanding several steps including detection, fiducial points detections, and similarity scoring.

In the next chapter, we will understand Recurrent Neural Networks and their use in Natural Language Processing problems. Later, we will use language models combined with image models for the captioning of images. We will visit several algorithms for this problem and see an implementation of two different types of data.

7
Image Captioning

In this chapter, we will deal with the problem of captioning images. This involves detecting the objects and also coming up with a text caption for the image. Image captioning also can be called **Image to Text translation**. Once thought a very tough problem, we have reasonably good results on this now. For this chapter, a dataset of images with corresponding captions is required. In this chapter, we will discuss the techniques and applications of image captioning in detail.

We will cover the following topics in this chapter:

- Understand the different datasets and metrics used to evaluate them
- Understand some techniques used for natural language processing problems
- Different words for vector models
- Several algorithms for image captioning
- Adverse results and scope for improvement

Understanding the problem and datasets

The process of automatically generating captions for images is a key deep learning task, as it combines the two worlds of language and vision. The uniqueness of the problem makes it one of the primary problems in computer vision. A deep learning model for image captioning should be able to identify the objects present in the image and also generate text in natural language expressing the relationship between the objects and actions. There are few datasets for this problem. The most famous of the datasets is an extension of the COCO dataset covered in object detection in Chapter 4, *Object Detection*.

Understanding natural language processing for image captioning

As natural language has to be generated from the image, getting familiar with **natural language processing (NLP)** becomes important. The concept of NLP is a vast subject, and hence we will limit our scope to topics that are relevant to image captioning. One form of natural language is **text**. The text is a sequence of words or characters. The atomic element of text is called **token**, which is a sequence of **characters**. A character is an atomic element of text.

In order to process any natural language in the form of text, the text has to be preprocessed by removing punctuation, brackets and so on. Then, the text has to be tokenized into words by separating them into spaces. Then, the words have to be converted to vectors. Next, we will see how this vector conversion can help.

Expressing words in vector form

Words expressed in vector form can help perform arithmetic operations on themselves. The vector has to be compact, with less dimension. Synonyms should have similar vectors and antonyms should have a different vector. Words can be converted to vectors so that relations can be compared as shown here:

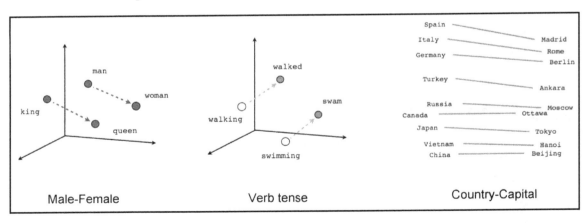

This vector arithmetic enables comparison in semantic space between different entities. Next, we will see how to create a deep learning model that can convert words to a vector representation.

Converting words to vectors

The words can be converted to vectors by training a model on a large text corpus. The model is trained such that given a word, the model can predict nearby words. The words are first one-hot encoded followed by hidden layers before predicting the one-hot encoding of nearby words. Training this way will create a compact representation of words. The context of the word can be obtained in two ways, as shown here:

- **Skip-gram**: Given a single word, try to predict few words that are close to
- **Continuous Bag Of Words** (**CBOW**): Reverse of skip-gram by predicting a word given a group of words

The following image illustrates these processes:

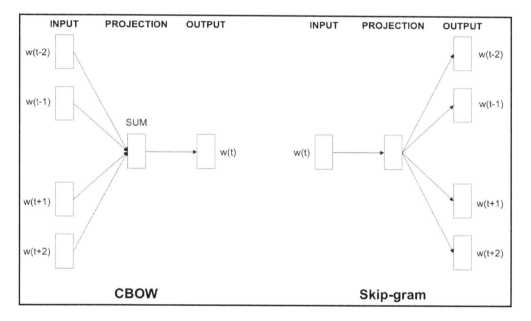

Both methods show good results. The words are converted to vectors in an embedding space. Next, we will see the details of training an embedding space.

Training an embedding

The embedding can be trained with a model the one shown here:

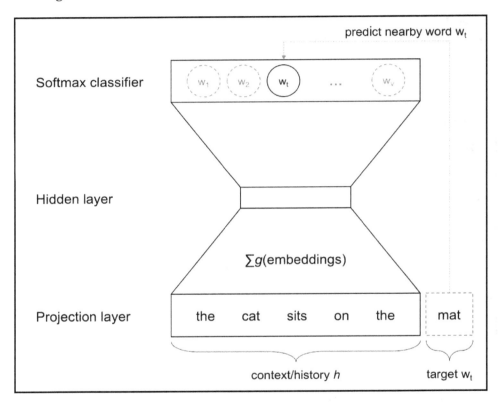

As shown in the preceding image, the target word is predicted based on context or history. The prediction is based on the **Softmax classifier**. The hidden layer learns the embedding as a compact representation. Note that this is not a full deep learning model, but it still works well. Here is a low dimensional visualization of the embedding:

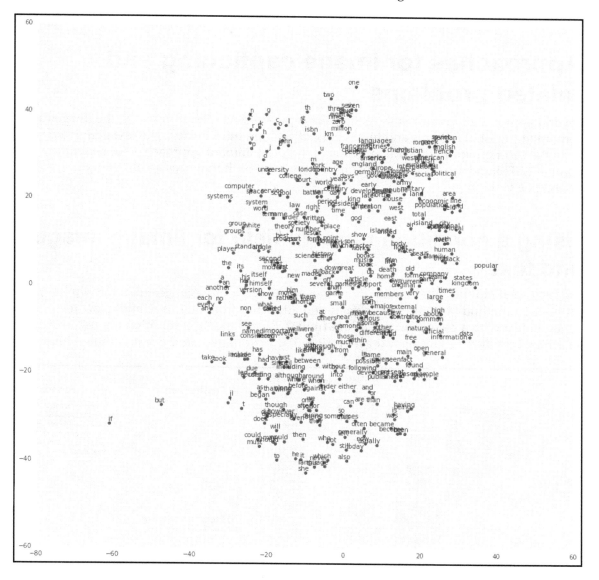

Low dimensional visualization of the embedding using Softmax classifier

This visualization is generated using TensorBoard. The words with similar semantic meanings or different parts of speech appear together.

We have learned how to train a compact representation for text to be used for generation. Next, we will see approaches for image captioning.

Approaches for image captioning and related problems

Several approaches have been suggested for captioning images. Intuitively, the images are converted to visual features and text is generated from the features. The text generated will be in the form of word embedding. Some of the predominant approaches for generating text involve LSTM and attention. Let's begin with an approach that uses an old way of generating text.

Using a condition random field for linking image and text

Kulkarni et al., in the paper http://www.tamaraberg.com/papers/generation_cvpr11.pdf, proposed a method of finding the objects and attributes from an image and using it to generate text with a **conditional random field** (**CRF**). The CRF is traditionally used for a structured prediction such as text generation. The flow of generating text is shown here:

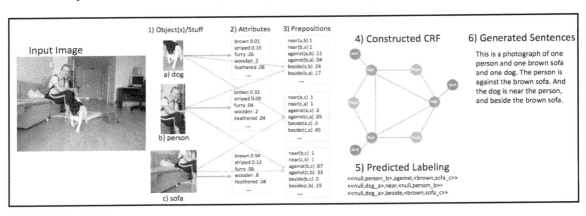

Figure illustrating the process of text generation using CRF [Reproduced from Kulkarni et al.]

The use of CRF has limitations in generating text in a coherent manner with proper placement of prepositions. The results are shown here:

Reproduced from Kulkarni et al.

The results have proper predictions of objects and attributes but fail at generating good descriptions.

Using RNN on CNN features to generate captions

Vinyals et al., in the paper `https://arxiv.org/pdf/1411.4555.pdf`, proposed an end to end trainable deep learning for image captioning, which has CNN and RNN stacked back to back. This is an end to end trainable model. The structure is shown here:

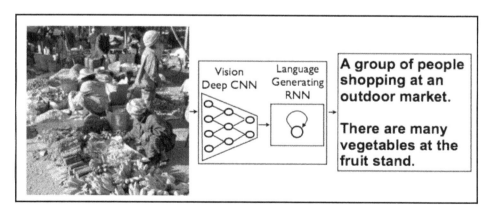

Reproduced from Vinyals et al. (2015)

This model could generate a sentence that is completed in natural language. The expanded view of the CNN and **LSTM** is shown here:

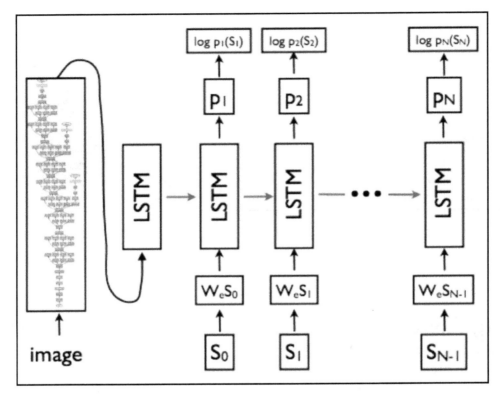

Figure illustrating the CNN AND LSTM architecture [Reproduced from Vinyals et al.]

This is an unrolled view of **LSTM**. A selective set of results is shown here:

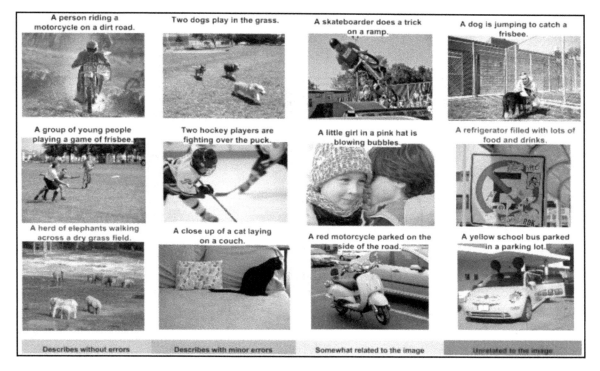

Reproduced from Vinyals et al. (2015)

In this process, the CNN encodes the image into features from which an RNN generates a sentence.

Creating captions using image ranking

Ordonez et al., in the paper `http://papers.nips.cc/paper/4470-im2text-describing-images-using-1-million-captioned-photographs.pdf`, proposed a method to rank the images followed by generating captions. The flow of this process is shown here:

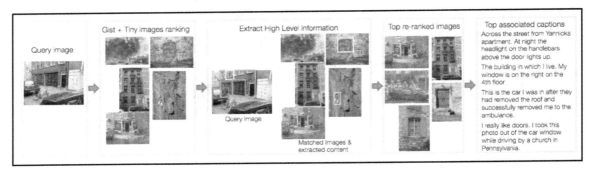

Reproduced from Ordonez et al. (2015)

The high-level information extracted from the ranked images can be used to generate the text. The following image shows that the more images that are available for ranking, the better the results will be:

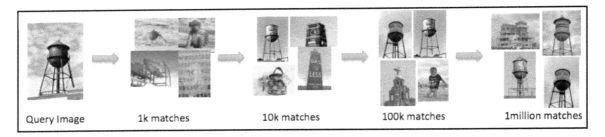

Reproduced from Ordonez et al. (2015)

Retrieving captions from images and images from captions

Chen et al., in the paper `https://www.cs.cmu.edu/~xinleic/papers/cvpr15_rnn.pdf`, proposed a method to retrieve images from text and text from images. This is a bi-directional mapping. The following image shows a person explaining an image in natural language and another person visually thinking about it:

Reproduced from Chen et al. (2015)

Retrieving captions can be achieved by connecting encoders of image and text through a latent space as shown here:

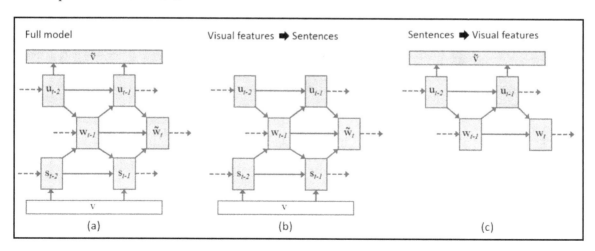

Reproduced from Chen et al. (2015)

The first model in the image is the full model used for training. Visual features can also be used to generate sentences, or vice-versa, as shown in the image.

Dense captioning

Johnson et al., in the paper `https://www.cv-foundation.org/openaccess/content_cvpr_2016/papers/Johnson_DenseCap_Fully_Convolutional_CVPR_2016_paper.pdf`, proposed a method for dense captioning. First, let's see some results, to understand the task:

two men standing on the beach. the sign is black and white. a girl holding a frisbee. a wooden sign. white sign with black writing. man holding a white frisbee. white frisbee in the air. the shorts are blue. a metal pole holding a sign. the sign is yellow.

Reproduced from Johnson et al.

As you can see, separate captions are generated for objects and actions in the image; hence the name; **dense captioning**. Here is the architecture proposed by Johnson et al.:

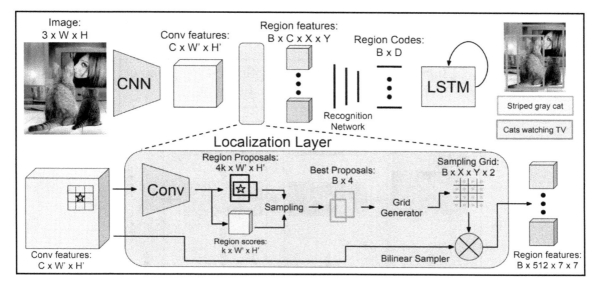

Reproduced from Johnson et al.

The architecture is essentially a combination of Faster-RCNN and **LSTM**. The region is generated producing the object detection results, and the visual features of the regions are used to generate the captions.

Using RNN for captioning

Donahue et al., in the paper `https://arxiv.org/pdf/1411.4389.pdf`, proposed **Long-term recurrent convolutional architectures** (**LRCN**) for the task of image captioning. The architecture of this model is shown here:

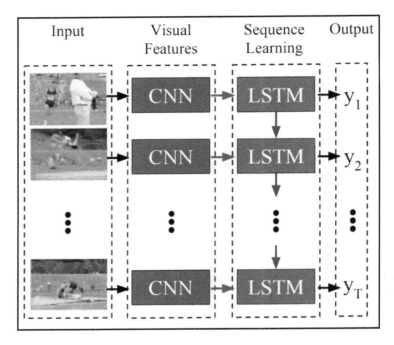

Reproduced from Donahue et al.

Both the CNN and LSTM is shown in the figure share weights across time, which makes this method scalable to arbitrarily long sequences.

Using multimodal metric space

Mao et al., in the paper `https://arxiv.org/pdf/1412.6632.pdf`, proposed a method that uses **multimodal embedding space** to generate the captions. The following figure illustrates this approach:

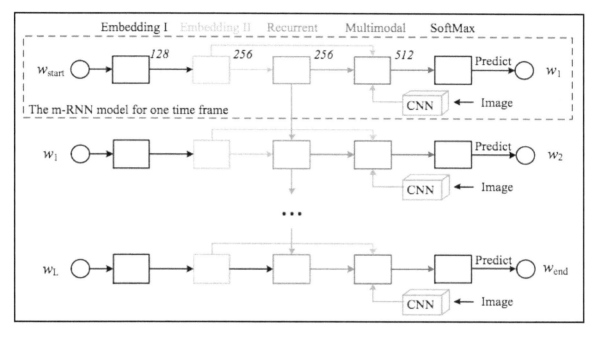

Reproduced from Mao et al.

Kiros et al., in the paper `https://arxiv.org/pdf/1411.2539.pdf`, proposed another multimodal approach to generate captions, which can embed both image and text into the same multimodal space. The following figure illustrates this approach:

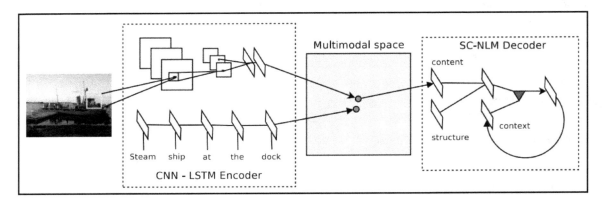

Reproduced from Kiros et al.

Both of the multimodal approaches give good results.

Using attention network for captioning

Xu et al., in the paper, `https://arxiv.org/pdf/1502.03044.pdf`, proposed a method for image captioning using an **attention mechanism**. The attention mechanism gives more weight to certain regions of the image than others. Attention also enables visualization, showing us where the model is focusing when it generates the next word. The proposed model is shown here:

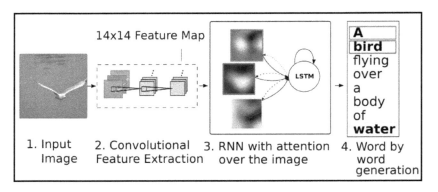

Reproduced from Xu et al.

First, CNN features are extracted from the image. Then, RNN with attention is applied to the image from which the words are generated.

Knowing when to look

Lu et al. (`https://arxiv.org/pdf/1612.01887.pdf`) proposed a method with attention, providing superior results. Know when to look at what region captured by attention gives better results. The flow is shown here:

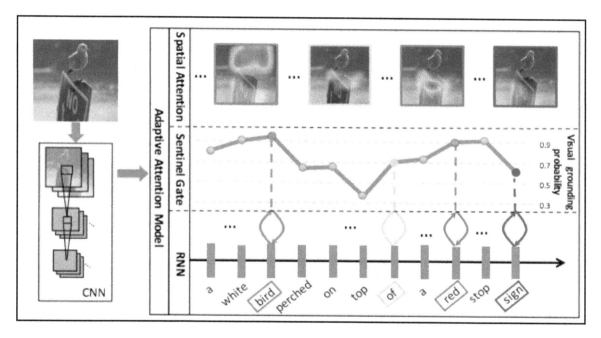

Reproduced from Lu et al.

The attention mechanism is shown here:

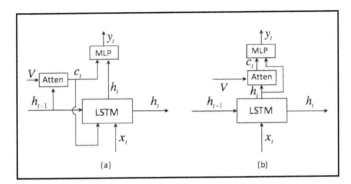

Reproduced from Lu et al.

The results, with regions that were paid attention to, are highlighted here:

Reproduced from Lu et al.

The unrolling of attention while generating captions is visualized here:

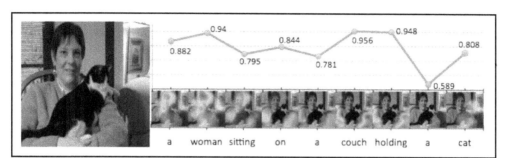

Reproduced from Lu et al.

We have seen several approaches for generating captions. Next, we will see an implementation.

Implementing attention-based image captioning

Let's define a CNN from VGG and the LSTM model, using the following code:

```
vgg_model = tf.keras.applications.vgg16.VGG16(weights='imagenet',
                                              include_top=False,
                                              input_tensor=input_tensor,
                                              input_shape=input_shape)

word_embedding = tf.keras.layers.Embedding(
    vocabulary_size, embedding_dimension, input_length=sequence_length)
embbedding = word_embedding(previous_words)
embbedding = tf.keras.layers.Activation('relu')(embbedding)
embbedding = tf.keras.layers.Dropout(dropout_prob)(embbedding)

cnn_features_flattened = tf.keras.layers.Reshape((height * height,
shape))(cnn_features)
net = tf.keras.layers.GlobalAveragePooling1D()(cnn_features_flattened)

net = tf.keras.layers.Dense(embedding_dimension, activation='relu')(net)
net = tf.keras.layers.Dropout(dropout_prob)(net)
net = tf.keras.layers.RepeatVector(sequence_length)(net)
net = tf.keras.layers.concatenate()([net, embbedding])
net = tf.keras.layers.Dropout(dropout_prob)(net)
```

Now, as we have defined the CNN, let's define the attention layer next, using the following code:

```
h_out_linear = tf.keras.layers.Convolution1D(
    depth, 1, activation='tanh', border_mode='same')(h)
h_out_linear = tf.keras.layers.Dropout(
    dropout_prob)(h_out_linear)
h_out_embed = tf.keras.layers.Convolution1D(
    embedding_dimension, 1, border_mode='same')(h_out_linear)
z_h_embed = tf.keras.layers.TimeDistributed(
    tf.keras.layers.RepeatVector(num_vfeats))(h_out_embed)

Vi = tf.keras.layers.Convolution1D(
    depth, 1, border_mode='same', activation='relu')(V)

Vi = tf.keras.layers.Dropout(dropout_prob)(Vi)
Vi_emb = tf.keras.layers.Convolution1D(
    embedding_dimension, 1, border_mode='same', activation='relu')(Vi)

z_v_linear = tf.keras.layers.TimeDistributed(
    tf.keras.layers.RepeatVector(sequence_length))(Vi)
z_v_embed = tf.keras.layers.TimeDistributed(
    tf.keras.layers.RepeatVector(sequence_length))(Vi_emb)

z_v_linear = tf.keras.layers.Permute((2, 1, 3))(z_v_linear)
z_v_embed = tf.keras.layers.Permute((2, 1, 3))(z_v_embed)

fake_feat = tf.keras.layers.Convolution1D(
    depth, 1, activation='relu', border_mode='same')(s)
fake_feat = tf.keras.layers.Dropout(dropout_prob)(fake_feat)

fake_feat_embed = tf.keras.layers.Convolution1D(
    embedding_dimension, 1, border_mode='same')(fake_feat)
z_s_linear = tf.keras.layers.Reshape((sequence_length, 1,
depth))(fake_feat)
z_s_embed = tf.keras.layers.Reshape(
    (sequence_length, 1, embedding_dimension))(fake_feat_embed)

z_v_linear = tf.keras.layers.concatenate(axis=-2)([z_v_linear, z_s_linear])
z_v_embed = tf.keras.layers.concatenate(axis=-2)([z_v_embed, z_s_embed])

z = tf.keras.layers.Merge(mode='sum')([z_h_embed, z_v_embed])
z = tf.keras.layers.Dropout(dropout_prob)(z)
z = tf.keras.layers.TimeDistributed(
    tf.keras.layers.Activation('tanh'))(z)
attention= tf.keras.layers.TimeDistributed(
    tf.keras.layers.Convolution1D(1, 1, border_mode='same'))(z)
```

```
attention = tf.keras.layers.Reshape((sequence_length,
num_vfeats))(attention)
attention = tf.keras.layers.TimeDistributed(
    tf.keras.layers.Activation('softmax'))(attention)
attention = tf.keras.layers.TimeDistributed(
    tf.keras.layers.RepeatVector(depth))(attention)
attention = tf.keras.layers.Permute((1,3,2))(attention)
w_Vi = tf.keras.layers.Add()([attention,z_v_linear])
sumpool = tf.keras.layers.Lambda(lambda x: K.sum(x, axis=-2),
                output_shape=(depth,))
c_vec = tf.keras.layers.TimeDistributed(sumpool)(w_Vi)
atten_out = tf.keras.layers.Merge(mode='sum')([h_out_linear,c_vec])
h = tf.keras.layers.TimeDistributed(
tf.keras.layers.Dense(embedding_dimension,activation='tanh'))(atten_out)
h = tf.keras.layers.Dropout(dropout_prob)(h)

predictions = tf.keras.layers.TimeDistributed(
    tf.keras.layers.Dense(vocabulary_size, activation='softmax'))(h)
```

With the help of the preceding code, we have defined a deep learning model that combines the CNN features with RNN with the help of an attention mechanism. This is currently the best method for generating captions.

Summary

In this chapter, we have understood the problems associated with image captions. We saw a few techniques involving natural language processing and various word2vec models such as GLOVE. We understood several algorithms such as CNN2RNN, metric learning, and combined objective. Later, we implemented a model that combines CNN and LSTM.

In the next chapter, we will come to understand generative models. We will learn and implement style algorithms from scratch and cover a few of the best models. We will also cover the cool **Generative Adversarial Networks** (**GAN**) and its various applications.

8
Generative Models

Generative models have become an important application in computer vision. Unlike the applications discussed in previous chapters that made predictions from images, generative models can create an image for specific objectives. In this chapter, we will understand:

- The applications of generative models
- Algorithms for style transfer
- Training a model for super-resolution of images
- Implementation and training of generative models
- Drawbacks of current models

By the end of the chapter, you will be able to implement some great applications for transferring style and understand the possibilities, as well as difficulties, associated with generative models.

Applications of generative models

Let's start this chapter with the possible applications of generative models. The applications are enormous. We will see a few of these applications to understand the motivation and possibilities.

Artistic style transfer

Artistic style transfer is the process of transferring the style of art to any image. For example, an image can be created with the artistic style of an image and content of another image. An example of one image combined with several different styles is shown here illustrated by Gatys et al. (`https://www.cv-foundation.org/openaccess/content_cvpr_2016/papers/Gatys_Image_Style_Transfer_CVPR_2016_paper.pdf`). The image **A** is the photo on which the style is applied, and the results are shown in other images:

Reproduced from Gatys et al.

This application has caught the public's attention, and there are several mobile apps in the market providing this facility.

Predicting the next frame in a video

Predicting future frames from synthetic video sets is possible using generative models. In the following image proposed by Lotter et al. (`https://arxiv.org/pdf/1511.06380.pdf`) the images on the left side are the models from the previous frame, and on the right side, there are two algorithms compared with respect to the ground truth:

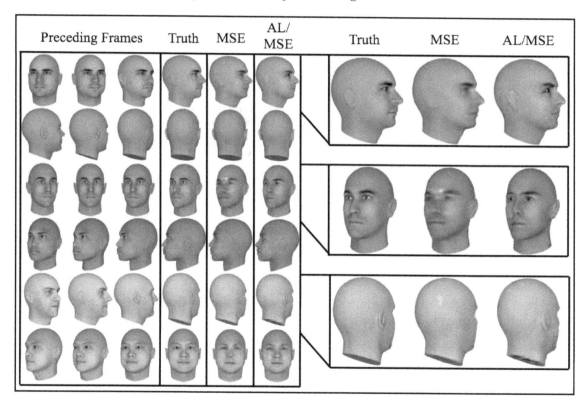

Reproduced from Lotter et al.

 The frames generated by the generative models will be realistic.

Super-resolution of images

The **super-resolution** is the process of creating higher resolution images from a smaller image. Traditionally, interpolations were used to create such bigger images. But interpolation misses the high-frequency details by giving a smoothened effect. Generative models that are trained for this specific purpose of super-resolution create images with excellent details. The following is an example of such models as proposed by Ledig et al. (https://arxiv.org/pdf/1609.04802.pdf). The left side is generated with **4x scaling** and looks indistinguishable from the original on the right:

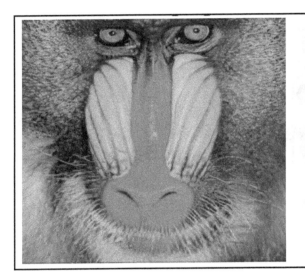

Reproduced from Ledig et al.

Super-resolution is useful for rendering a low-resolution image on a high-quality display or print. Another application could be a reconstruction of compressed images with good quality.

Interactive image generation

Generative models can be used to create images by **interaction**. A user can add edits and the images can be generated, reflecting the edits as shown here as proposed by Zhu et al. (`https://arxiv.org/pdf/1609.03552v2.pdf`):

Reproduced from Zhu et al.

As shown, the images are generated based on the shape and color of the edits. A green color stroke at the bottom creates a grassland, a rectangle creates a skyscraper and so on. The images will be generated and fine-tuned with further inputs from the user. The generated image can also be used to retrieve the most similar real image that can be utilized. Interactive image generation provides an entirely new way of searching images intuitively.

Image to image translation

An image can be used to generate other images with specific objectives, and hence this process is called **an image to image translation**. A few examples of such translations are shown here with their corresponding criteria as propose by Isola et al. (`https://arxiv.org/pdf/1611.07004.pdf`):

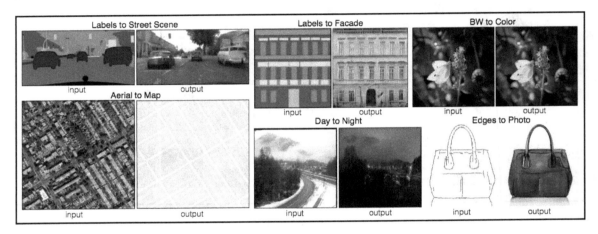

Reproduced from Isola et al.

A drawing with a label can be converted to a realistic image for creative purposes. A black and white image can be translated to a color image. Such translations are useful for photo editing apps, coloring old movies, fashion design and so on.

Text to image generation

Images can be generated from text descriptions, and the steps for this are similar to the image to image translation. Here are a few examples that are generated from a natural text description shown by Reed at al. (`https://arxiv.org/pdf/1605.05396.pdf`):

 Currently, this model works for only a few objects. Image generation from a text is not yet realistic enough to be used in applications.

Inpainting

Inpainting is the process of filling a gap within the image, as shown here:

Source: https://www.flickr.com/photos/littleredelf/4756059924/

The image on the left is the normal image and the one on the right is the processed image. As you can see from the image, the unwanted things are removed from the picture. Inpainting is useful for removing unwanted objects from the image, and also for filling in the space of scanned artwork.

Blending

Blending is the process of pasting a part of an image over another image smoothly, without any artefacts. The image **a** shown here shows a case where one image is placed on another, which gives a bad impression. The images **b** and **c** represent the conventional blending techniques such as the **modified Poisson method** and a **multi-spline method**, respectively.

The final image, or the image **d**, shows the results of a generative method of blending which gives a much better result than the other methods as shown by Wu et al. (`https://arxiv.org/pdf/1703.07195.pdf`):

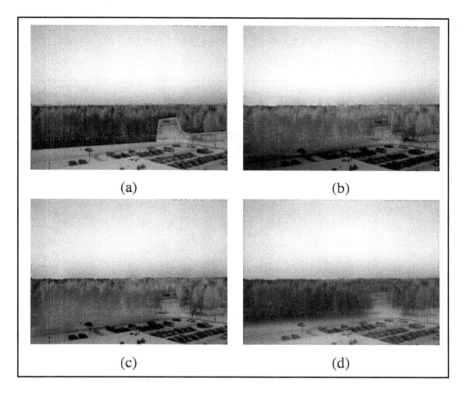

Reproduced from Wu et al.

 Blending is very useful in photo editing and for special effects in the movie industry.

Transforming attributes

The attributes of images can be changed using generative models. A person's face could be modified to reflect different attributes such as gender, glasses, age, and so on, as shown here by Lample et al. (`https://research.fb.com/wp-content/uploads/2017/11/fader_networks__conditional_attribute_based_image_generation_by_disentangling_in_latent_space.pdf`):

Reproduced with Lample et al.

Changing the attributes can be used for creative applications as well as for fun, and can also be used for generating more training data with variations.

Creating training data

Generative models can be used for generating training at a larger scale and can even be used to refine the synthetic images created for training. Here are the synthetic images created for traffic sign recognition, using generative models as shown by Wang et al. (`https://arxiv.org/pdf/1707.03124.pdf`)

Reproduced from Wang et al.

 Using these images makes the classifications more accurate.

Creating new animation characters

Generative models can be used for creating new animation characters with various conditions such as facial expressions, hairstyles, costumes, and so on, as shown by Jin et al. (`https://arxiv.org/pdf/1708.05509.pdf`):

Reproduced from Jin et al.

Creating new characters with different attributes could revolutionize the animation industry.

3D models from photos

We can create 3D models from 2D images by using generative models, as shown by Wu et al. (`https://arxiv.org/pdf/1610.07584.pdf`):

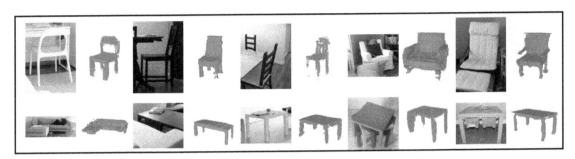

Reproduced from Wu et al.

Creating 3D models from images is useful for robotics, augmented reality and in animation industries. We will learn the algorithms behind them in the following sections. In the next section, we will implement neural artistic style transfer.

Neural artistic style transfer

The first application we will implement is the **neural artistic style transfer**. Here, we will transfer the style of **Van Gogh** art onto an image. An image can be considered as a combination of style and content. The artistic style transfer technique transforms an image to look like a painting with a specific painting style. We will see how to code this idea up. The `loss` function will compare the generated image with the content of the photo and style of the painting. Hence, the optimization is carried out for the image pixel, rather than for the weights of the network. Two values are calculated by comparing the content of the photo with the generated image followed by the style of the painting and the generated image.

Content loss

Since pixels are not a good choice, we will use the CNN features of various layers, as they are a better representation of the content. The initial layers as seen in `Chapter 3`, *Image Retrieval*, have high-frequency such as edges, corners, and textures but the later layers represent objects, and hence are better for content. The latter layer can compare the *object to object* better than the pixel. But for this, we need to first import the required libraries, using the following code:

```
import numpy as np
from PIL import Image
from scipy.optimize import fmin_l_bfgs_b
from scipy.misc import imsave
from vgg16_avg import VGG16_Avg
from keras import metrics
from keras.models import Model
from keras import backend as K
```

Now, let's load the required image, using the following command:

```
content_image = Image.open(work_dir + 'bird_orig.png')
```

We will use the following image for this instance:

As we are using the VGG architecture for extracting the features, the mean of all the `ImageNet` images has to be subtracted from all the images, as shown in the following code:

```
imagenet_mean = np.array([123.68, 116.779, 103.939], dtype=np.float32)


def subtract_imagenet_mean(image):
    return (image - imagenet_mean)[:, :, :, ::-1]
```

Note that the channels are different. The `preprocess` function takes the generated image and subtracts the mean and then reverses the channel. The `deprocess` function reverses that effect because of the preprocessing step, as shown in the following code:

```
def add_imagenet_mean(image, s):
    return np.clip(image.reshape(s)[:, :, :, ::-1] + imagenet_mean, 0, 255)
```

First, we will see how to create an image with the content from another image. This is a process of creating an image from **random noise**. The content used here is the sum of the **activation** in some layer. We will minimize the loss of the content between the random noise and image, which is termed as the content loss. This loss is similar to pixel-wise loss but applied on layer activations, hence will capture the content leaving out the noise. Any CNN architecture can be used to do forward inference of content image and random noise. The activations are taken and the mean squared error is calculated, comparing the activations of these two outputs.

The pixel of the random image is updated while the CNN weights are frozen. We will freeze the VGG network for this case. Now, the VGG model can be loaded. Generative images are very sensitive to subsampling techniques such as **max pooling**. Getting back the pixel values from max pooling is not possible. Hence, **average pooling** is a smoother method than max pooling. The function to convert VGG model with average pooling is used for loading the model, as shown here:

```
vgg_model = VGG16_Avg(include_top=False)
```

Note that the weights are the same for this model as the original, even though the pooling type has been changed. The ResNet and Inception models are not suited for this because of their inability to provide various abstractions. We will take the activations from the last convolutional layer of the VGG model namely `block_conv1`, while the model was frozen. This is the third last layer from the VGG, with a wide receptive field. The code for the same is given here for your reference:

```
content_layer = vgg_model.get_layer('block5_conv1').output
```

Now, a new model is created with a truncated VGG, till the layer that was giving good features. Hence, the image can be loaded now and can be used to carry out the forward inference, to get the **actually activated layers**. A TensorFlow variable is created to capture the activation, using the following code:

```
content_model = Model(vgg_model.input, content_layer)
content_image_array =
subtract_imagenet_mean(np.expand_dims(np.array(content_image), 0))
content_image_shape = content_image_array.shape
target = K.variable(content_model.predict(content_image_array))
```

Let's define an evaluator class to compute the loss and gradients of the image. The following class returns the loss and gradient values at any point of the iteration:

```
class ConvexOptimiser(object):
    def __init__(self, cost_function, tensor_shape):
        self.cost_function = cost_function
        self.tensor_shape = tensor_shape
        self.gradient_values = None

    def loss(self, point):
        loss_value, self.gradient_values =
self.cost_function([point.reshape(self.tensor_shape)])
        return loss_value.astype(np.float64)

    def gradients(self, point):
        return self.gradient_values.flatten().astype(np.float64)
```

Loss function can be defined as the mean squared error between the values of activations at specific convolutional layers. The loss will be computed between the layers of generated image and the original content photo, as shown here:

```
mse_loss = metrics.mean_squared_error(content_layer, target)
```

The gradients of the loss can be computed by considering the input of the model, as shown:

```
grads = K.gradients(mse_loss, vgg_model.input)
```

The input to the function is the input of the model and the output will be the array of loss and gradient values as shown:

```
cost_function = K.function([vgg_model.input], [mse_loss]+grads)
```

This function is deterministic to optimize, and hence **SGD** is not required:

```
optimiser = ConvexOptimiser(cost_function, content_image_shape)
```

This function can be optimized using a simple optimizer, as it is convex and hence is deterministic. We can also save the image at every step of the iteration. We will define it in such a way that the gradients are accessible, as we are using the scikit-learn's optimizer, for the final optimization. Note that this loss function is convex and so, a simple optimizer is good enough for the computation. The optimizer can be defined using the following code:

```
def optimise(optimiser, iterations, point, tensor_shape, file_name):
    for i in range(iterations):
        point, min_val, info = fmin_l_bfgs_b(optimiser.loss,
point.flatten(),
                                fprime=optimiser.gradients, maxfun=20)
        point = np.clip(point, -127, 127)
        print('Loss:', min_val)
        imsave(work_dir + 'gen_'+file_name+'_{i}.png',
add_imagenet_mean(point.copy(), tensor_shape)[0])
    return point
```

The optimizer takes `loss` function, point, and gradients, and returns the updates. A random image needs to be generated so that the content loss will be minimized, using the following code:

```
def generate_rand_img(shape):
    return np.random.uniform(-2.5, 2.5, shape)/1
generated_image = generate_rand_img(content_image_shape)
```

Here is the random image that is created:

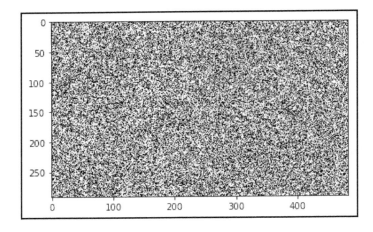

The optimization can be run for 10 iterations to see the results, as shown:

```
iterations = 10
generated_image = optimise(optimiser, iterations, generated_image,
content_image_shape, 'content')
```

If everything goes well, the loss should print as shown here, over the iterations:

```
Current loss value: 73.2010421753
Current loss value: 22.7840042114
Current loss value: 12.6585302353
Current loss value: 8.53817081451
Current loss value: 6.64649534225
Current loss value: 5.56395864487
Current loss value: 4.83072710037
Current loss value: 4.32800722122
Current loss value: 3.94804215431
Current loss value: 3.66387653351
```

Here is the image that is generated and now, it almost looks like a bird. The optimization can be run for further iterations to have this done:

An optimizer took the image and updated the pixels so that the content is the same. Though the results are worse, it can reproduce the image to a certain extent with the content. All the images through iterations give a good intuition on how the image is generated. There is no batching involved in this process. In the next section, we will see how to create an image in the style of a painting.

Style loss using the Gram matrix

After creating an image that has the content of the original image, we will see how to create an image with just the style. Style can be thought of as a mix of colour and texture of an image. For that purpose, we will define style loss. First, we will load the image and convert it to an array, as shown in the following code:

```
style_image = Image.open(work_dir + 'starry_night.png')
style_image = style_image.resize(np.divide(style_image.size,
3.5).astype('int32'))
```

Here is the style image we have loaded:

Now, we will preprocess this image by changing the channels, by using the following code:

```
style_image_array = subtract_imagenet_mean(np.expand_dims(style_image,
0)[:, :, :, :3])
style_image_shape = style_image_array.shape
```

For this purpose, we will consider several layers, like we have done in the following code:

```
model = VGG16_Avg(include_top=False, input_shape=shp[1:])
outputs = {l.name: l.output for l in model.layers}
```

Now, we will take multiple layers as an array output of the first four blocks, using the following code:

```
layers = [outputs['block{}_conv1'.format(o)] for o in range(1,3)]
```

A new model is now created, that can output all those layers and assign the target variables, using the following code:

```
layers_model = Model(model.input, layers)
targs = [K.variable(o) for o in layers_model.predict(style_arr)]
```

Style loss is calculated using the **Gram matrix**. The Gram matrix is the product of a matrix and its transpose. The activation values are simply transposed and multiplied. This matrix is then used for computing the error between the style and random images. The Gram matrix loses the location information but will preserve the texture information. We will define the Gram matrix using the following code:

```
def grammian_matrix(matrix):
    flattened_matrix = K.batch_flatten(K.permute_dimensions(matrix, (2, 0,
1)))
    matrix_transpose_dot = K.dot(flattened_matrix,
K.transpose(flattened_matrix))
    element_count = matrix.get_shape().num_elements()
    return matrix_transpose_dot / element_count
```

As you might be aware now, it is a measure of the correlation between the pair of columns. The height and width dimensions are flattened out. This doesn't include any local pieces of information, as the coordinate information is disregarded. Style loss computes the mean squared error between the Gram matrix of the input image and the target, as shown in the following code:

```
def style_mse_loss(x, y):
    return metrics.mse(grammian_matrix(x), grammian_matrix(y))
```

Now, let's compute the loss by summing up all the activations from the various layers, using the following code:

```
style_loss = sum(style_mse_loss(l1[0], l2[0]) for l1, l2 in
zip(style_features, style_targets))
grads = K.gradients(style_loss, vgg_model.input)
style_fn = K.function([vgg_model.input], [style_loss]+grads)
optimiser = ConvexOptimiser(style_fn, style_image_shape)
```

We then solve it as the same way we did before, by creating a random image. But this time, we will also apply a Gaussian filter, as shown in the following code:

```
generated_image = generate_rand_img(style_image_shape)
```

The random image generated will look like this:

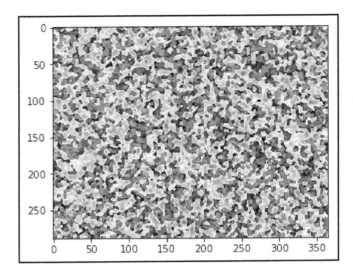

The optimization can be run for 10 iterations to see the results, as shown below:

```
generated_image = optimise(optimiser, iterations, generated_image,
style_image_shape)
```

If everything goes well, the solver should print the loss values similar to the following:

```
Current loss value: 5462.45556641
Current loss value: 189.738555908
Current loss value: 82.4192581177
Current loss value: 55.6530838013
Current loss value: 37.215713501
Current loss value: 24.4533748627
Current loss value: 15.5914745331
Current loss value: 10.9425945282
Current loss value: 7.66888141632
Current loss value: 5.84042310715
```

Here is the image that is generated:

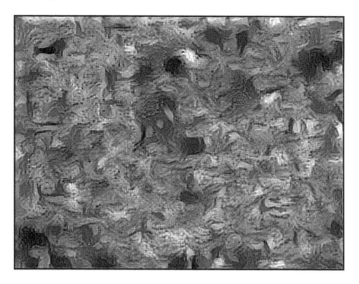

Here, from a random noise, we have created an image with a particular painting style without any location information. In the next section, we will see how to combine both—the content and style loss.

Style transfer

Now we know how to reconstruct an image, as well as how to construct an image that captures the style of an original image. The obvious idea may be to just combine these two approaches by weighting and adding the two `loss` functions, as shown in the following code:

```
w,h = style.size
src = img_arr[:,:h,:w]
```

Like before, we're going to grab a sequence of layer outputs to compute the style loss. However, we still only need one layer output to compute the content loss. How do we know which layer to grab? As we discussed earlier, the lower the layer, the more exact the content reconstruction will be. In merging content reconstruction with style, we might expect that a looser reconstruction of the content will allow more room for the style to affect (re: inspiration). Furthermore, a later layer ensures that the image looks like the same subject, even if it doesn't have the same details. The following code is used for this process:

```
style_layers = [outputs['block{}_conv2'.format(o)] for o in range(1,6)]
content_name = 'block4_conv2'
content_layer = outputs[content_name]
```

Now, a separate model for style is created with required output layers, using the following code:

```
style_model = Model(model.input, style_layers)
style_targs = [K.variable(o) for o in style_model.predict(style_arr)]
```

We will also create another model for the content with the content layer, using the following code:

```
content_model = Model(model.input, content_layer)
content_targ = K.variable(content_model.predict(src))
```

Now, the merging of the two approaches is as simple as merging their respective loss functions. Note that as opposed to our previous functions, this function is producing three separate types of outputs:

- One for the original image
- One for the image whose style we're emulating
- One for the random image whose pixels we are training

One way for us to tune how the reconstructions mix is by changing the factor on the content loss, which we have here as 1/10. If we increase that denominator, the style will have a larger effect on the image, and if it's too large, the original content of the image will be obscured by an unstructured style. Likewise, if it is too small then the image will not have enough style. We will use the following code for this process:

```
style_wgts = [0.05,0.2,0.2,0.25,0.3]
```

The `loss` function takes both style and content layers, as shown here:

```
loss = sum(style_loss(l1[0], l2[0])*w
           for l1,l2,w in zip(style_layers, style_targs, style_wgts))
loss += metrics.mse(content_layer, content_targ)/10
grads = K.gradients(loss, model.input)
transfer_fn = K.function([model.input], [loss]+grads)
evaluator = Evaluator(transfer_fn, shp)
```

We will run the solver for 10 iterations as before, using the following code:

```
iterations=10
x = rand_img(shp)
x = solve_image(evaluator, iterations, x)
```

The loss values should be printed as shown here:

```
Current loss value: 2557.953125
Current loss value: 732.533630371
Current loss value: 488.321166992
Current loss value: 385.827178955
Current loss value: 330.915924072
Current loss value: 293.238189697
Current loss value: 262.066864014
Current loss value: 239.34185791
Current loss value: 218.086700439
Current loss value: 203.045211792
```

These results are remarkable. Each one of them does a fantastic job of recreating the original image in the style of the artist. The generated image will look like the following:

We will now conclude the style transfer section. This operation is really slow but can work with any images. In the next section, we will see how to use a similar idea to create a super-resolution network. There are several ways to make this better, such as:

- Adding a Gaussian filter to a random image
- Adding different weights to the layers
- Different layers and weights can be used to content
- Initialization of image rather than random image
- Color can be preserved
- Masks can be used for specifying what is required
- Any sketch can be converted to painting
- Drawing a sketch and creating the image

 Any image can be converted to artistic style by training a CNN to output such an image.

Generative Adversarial Networks

Generative Adversarial Networks (**GAN**) were invented by **Ian Goodfellow**, in 2014. It is an unsupervised algorithm where two neural networks are trained as a discriminator and a generator, simultaneously. The technique can generate an image from random noise and a discriminator can evaluate whether is an original image. After further training, the generator network can generate photo-realistic images. The generator network is typically a deconvolutional neural network and the discriminator is a convolution neural network.

An excellent analogy to understand this is to think of the generator as someone who prints fake money and the discriminator as a police officer who determines whether the money is fake or not. The generator keeps improving the quality of the fake money based on the feedback from the police till the police can't differentiate between the original and fake money. Now, let's start with the implementation.

Vanilla GAN

The original GAN is called a **vanilla GAN**. Before we construct the model, let's define a few layers that will be useful for the rest of the chapter. The following is the `convolutional_layers` with leaky activations and regularization added:

```
def convolution_layer(input_layer,
                      filters,
                      kernel_size=[4, 4],
                      activation=tf.nn.leaky_relu):
    layer = tf.layers.conv2d(
        inputs=input_layer,
        filters=filters,
        kernel_size=kernel_size,
        activation=activation,
        kernel_regularizer=tf.nn.l2_loss,
        bias_regularizer=tf.nn.l2_loss,
    )
    add_variable_summary(layer, 'convolution')
    return layer
```

Next, we will define a `transpose_convolution_layer` that is the opposite of a `convolution_layer` with regularization, using the following code:

```
def transpose_convolution_layer(input_layer,
                                filters,
                                kernel_size=[4, 4],
                                activation=tf.nn.relu,
                                strides=2):
    layer = tf.layers.conv2d_transpose(
        inputs=input_layer,
        filters=filters,
        kernel_size=kernel_size,
        activation=activation,
        strides=strides,
        kernel_regularizer=tf.nn.l2_loss,
        bias_regularizer=tf.nn.l2_loss,
    )
    add_variable_summary(layer, 'convolution')
    return layer
```

Next, we will define a dense layer with non-linear activations, using the following code:

```
def dense_layer(input_layer,
                units,
                activation=tf.nn.relu):
    layer = tf.layers.dense(
        inputs=input_layer,
        units=units,
        activation=activation
    )
    add_variable_summary(layer, 'dense')
    return layer
```

Now, we will define a generator that takes noise as an input and changes into an image. The generator consists of a couple of fully connected layers followed by transpose convolution layers to upsample the noise. Finally, a convolution layer is presented to make the noise as a single channel. There are batch normalization layers between every layer for gradients to flow smoothly. We will use the following code to define the generator:

```
def get_generator(input_noise, is_training=True):
    generator = dense_layer(input_noise, 1024)
    generator = tf.layers.batch_normalization(generator,
training=is_training)
    generator = dense_layer(generator, 7 * 7 * 256)
    generator = tf.layers.batch_normalization(generator,
training=is_training)
    generator = tf.reshape(generator,  [-1, 7, 7, 256])
    generator = transpose_convolution_layer(generator, 64)
    generator = tf.layers.batch_normalization(generator,
training=is_training)
    generator = transpose_convolution_layer(generator, 32)
    generator = tf.layers.batch_normalization(generator,
training=is_training)
    generator = convolution_layer(generator, 3)
    generator = convolution_layer(generator, 1, activation=tf.nn.tanh)
    return generator
```

We will now define the **discriminator** part of the GAN that takes images and tries to distinguish fake from real images. The discriminator is a regular convolutional net with a few `convolutional_layers` followed by dense layers. Batch normalization layers are present in-between the layers. We will use the following code to define the discriminator:

```
def get_discriminator(image, is_training=True):
    x_input_reshape = tf.reshape(image, [-1, 28, 28, 1],
                                 name='input_reshape')
    discriminator = convolution_layer(x_input_reshape, 64)
    discriminator = convolution_layer(discriminator, 128)
    discriminator = tf.layers.flatten(discriminator)
    discriminator = dense_layer(discriminator, 1024)
    discriminator = tf.layers.batch_normalization(discriminator,
training=is_training)
    discriminator = dense_layer(discriminator, 2)
    return discriminator
```

After the discriminator is created, we will create a noise vector that will be the input to the generator, using the following code:

```
input_noise = tf.random_normal([batch_size, input_dimension])
```

The GAN model can be created with the `tf.contrib.gan` module in TensorFlow. It takes the generator and discriminator methods along with their corresponding inputs, as shown here:

```
gan = tf.contrib.gan.gan_model(
    get_generator,
    get_discriminator,
    real_images,
    input_noise)
```

Now, the training can be started with the `gan_train` method that takes the `gan_train_ops` method with loss and optimizers for the generator and discriminator, using the following code:

```
tf.contrib.gan.gan_train(
    tf.contrib.gan.gan_train_ops(
        gan,
        tf.contrib.gan.gan_loss(gan),
        tf.train.AdamOptimizer(0.001),
        tf.train.AdamOptimizer(0.0001)))
```

By running this, a GAN model is created that can output images from random vectors. The generated images are unconstrained and can be from any label. In the next section, we will use a conditional GAN to produce the output we want.

Conditional GAN

A conditional GAN generates images with a label that we want. For example, we can ask the model to produce the digit 8 and the model will produce an 8. To enable this, the labels are required along with noise to be trained with the model, as shown here:

```
gan = tf.contrib.gan.gan_model(
    get_generator,
    get_discriminator,
    real_images,
    (input_noise, labels))
```

The rest of the training is similar to that of the vanilla GAN. Next, we will use a GAN for compressing the images.

Adversarial loss

An adversarial loss is a loss from the generator. This loss can be combined with a pixel-wise loss between the fake and real images to form a combined adversarial loss. The GAN model has to be supplied with `real_images`, to both the generator and discriminator, as shown here:

```
gan = tf.contrib.gan.gan_model(
    get_autoencoder,
    get_discriminator,
    real_images,
    real_images)
```

The generator is an autoencoder. The implementation can be found in Chapter 3, *Image Retrieval*. After this, we will define the losses, using the following code:

```
loss = tf.contrib.gan.gan_loss(
    gan, gradient_penalty=1.0)

l1_pixel_loss = tf.norm(gan.real_data - gan.generated_data, ord=1)

loss = tf.contrib.gan.losses.combine_adversarial_loss(
    loss, gan, l1_pixel_loss, weight_factor=1)
```

The gradient of the GAN loss is penalized. Then, the pixel-wise loss is computed and added to the penalized loss. Training this model creates a powerful autoencoder, that can be used for image compression.

Image translation

An image can be translated to another image, as we have already learned in the application's section. The input images are given to the discriminator, whereas the target images are given to the generator while creating the GAN model as shown here:

```
gan = tf.contrib.gan.gan_model(
    get_generator,
    get_discriminator,
    real_images,
    input_images)
```

The least square loss is used for training, in addition to the pixel-wise loss to train the model. It can be calculated using the following code:

```
loss = tf.contrib.gan.gan_loss(
    gan,
    tf.contrib.gan.losses.least_squares_generator_loss,
    tf.contrib.gan.losses.least_squares_discriminator_loss)

l1_loss = tf.norm(gan.real_data - gan.generated_data, ord=1)

gan_loss = tf.contrib.gan.losses.combine_adversarial_loss(
    loss, gan, l1_loss, weight_factor=1)
```

Using this technique, an image can be translated to another image.

InfoGAN

InfoGAN can generate images of the required label without any explicit supervised training. The `infogan_model` takes unstructured and structured input, as shown in the following code:

```
info_gan = tf.contrib.gan.infogan_model(
    get_generator,
    get_discriminator,
    real_images,
    unstructured_input,
    structured_input)

loss = tf.contrib.gan.gan_loss(
    info_gan,
    gradient_penalty_weight=1,
    gradient_penalty_epsilon=1e-10,
    mutual_information_penalty_weight=1)
```

The loss is defined with a penalty as the training is unstable. Adding the penalty provides more stability during the training.

Drawbacks of GAN

The GAN generated images have some drawbacks such as counting, perspective, and global structures. This is currently being extensively researched to improve the models.

Visual dialogue model

The **visual dialogue model** (**VDM**) enables chat based on images. VDM applies technologies from computer vision, **Natural Language Processing** (**NLP**) and chatbots. It has found major applications such as explaining to blind people about images, to doctors about medical scans, virtual companions and so on. Next, we will see the algorithm to solve this challenge.

Algorithm for VDM

The algorithm discussed here is proposed by **Lu et al** (`https://research.fb.com/wp-content/uploads/2017/11/camera_ready_nips2017.pdf`). Lu et al proposed a GAN-based VDM. The generator generates answers and the discriminator ranks those answers. The following is a schematic representation of the process:

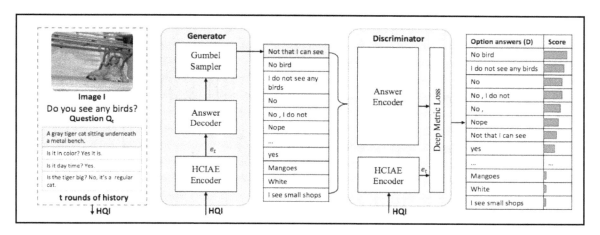

Architecture of the VDMs based on GAN techniques [Reproduced from Lu et al.]

The history of chat, the current question and image are fed as an input to the generator. Next, we will see how the generator works.

Generator

The generator has an encoder and decoder. The encoder takes an image, question, and history as inputs. The encoder first attends to the history from **LSTM** and attends to the output from the image. The flow is shown here:

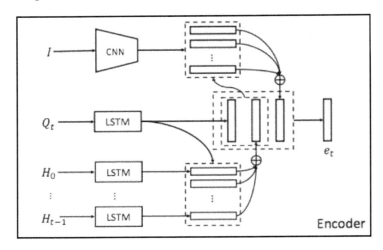

Reproduced from Lu et al.

The entire history is available and **LSTM** attends to the history of the chat. The output is attended by the image producing the embedding. The embedding generated by the encoder is used by the decoder to create an answer. The decoder is made of RNN. The encoder and decoder together form the generator producing the possible answers. Next, we will see how the discriminator works.

Discriminator

The discriminator takes the generated sequences from the generator and ranks them. The ranking is done with the embedding learned with an n-pair loss. The n-pair loss is similar to triplet loss except that several pairs of positive and negatives are used for comparison. Here are some of the results produced by the model.

Q: Is it a home or restaurant?
A: I think restaurant.
G-MLE: I can't tell.
Ours ($z1$): Hard to say.
Ours ($z2$): It looks like a restaurant.
Ours ($z3$): I can't tell because it is too close.

Q: Can you see his face?
A: I am not sure.
G-MLE: Yes.
Ours ($z1$): I can only see the back of his body.
Ours ($z2$): No.
Ours ($z3$): No , he's too far away.

Q: How old does the man seem to be?
A: 20's.
G-MLE: Late teens.
Ours ($z1$): On his 20s.
Ours ($z2$): In his twenties.
Ours ($z3$): Mid 20's.

Q: Can you see broccoli?
A: Yes, 3 larger pieces and some small.
G-MLE: No, just the broccoli.
Ours ($z1$): I can see broccoli, slightly butter.
Ours ($z2$): Yes, there is broccoli.
Ours ($z3$): Yes, broccoli is green.

Reproduced from Lu et al.

The results are reasonable and better than the results produced by a simple discriminator.

Summary

In this chapter, we have learned about generative models and the vast number of applications. We implemented them to transfer style from one to another while preserving the content. We saw the intuition behind GAN and trained models to do the same. In the end, we learned about the visual dialogue system.

In the next chapter, we will learn about deep learning methods for video analysis. We will see how to access video content through cameras, files, and so on. We will implement video classification by applying classification on a frame level and on the video as a whole. Later, we will see how to track objects in a video.

9
Video Classification

In this chapter, we will see how to train deep learning models for video data. We will start classifying videos on a frame basis. Then, we will use the temporal information for better accuracy. Later, we will extend the applications of images to videos, including pose estimation, captioning, and generating videos.

We will cover the following topics in this chapter:

- The datasets and the algorithms of video classification
- Splitting a video into frames and classifying videos
- Training a model for visual features on an individual frame level 0
- Understanding 3D convolution and its use in videos
- Incorporating motion vectors on video
- Object tracking utilizing the temporal information
- Applications such as human pose estimation and video captioning

Understanding and classifying videos

A video is nothing but a series of images. Video brings a new dimension to the image along the temporal direction. The spatial features of the images and temporal features of the video can be put together, providing a better outcome than just the image. The extra dimension also results in a lot of space and hence increases the complexity of training and inference. The computational demands are extremely high for processing a video. Video also changes the architecture of deep learning models as we have to consider the temporal features.

Video classification is the task of labeling a video with a category. A category can be on the frame level or for the whole video. There could be actions or tasks performed in the video. Hence, a video classification may label the objects present in the video or label the actions happening in the video. In the next section, we will see the available datasets for video classification tasks.

Exploring video classification datasets

Video classification is the major problem that is studied with video data. Several videos are taken and labelled with various objects or actions that are associated with the data. The datasets vary according to size, quality, and the type of labels. Some even include multiple labels for video. The videos are rather usually short in length. A long video may have various actions performed and hence can be segmented temporally, before classifying the cut video segments or snippets individually. Next, we will consider the details of some specific datasets.

UCF101

The **University of Central Florida** (**UCF101**) is a dataset for action recognition. The videos are collected on YouTube and consist of realistic actions. There are 101 action categories available in this dataset. There is another dataset called **UCF50** which has 50 categories. There are 13,320 videos in this dataset across the actions. The videos have a diversified variation of background, scale, pose, occlusion, and illumination conditions. The action categories are grouped into 25, which share similar variations such as the background, pose, scale, viewpoint, illumination and so on.

The actions and number of videos per action are shown here:

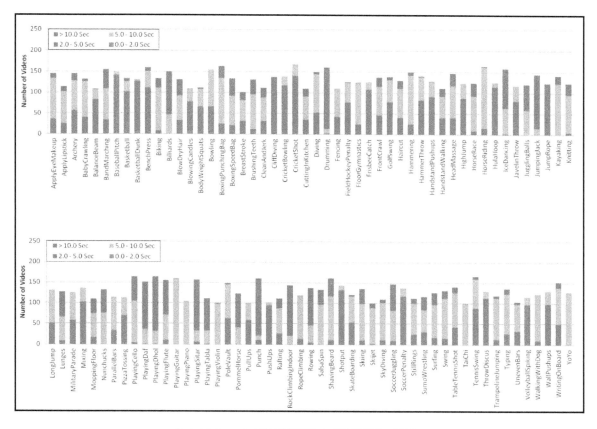

Source: http://crcv.ucf.edu/data/UCF101/Number%20of%20Videos%202.jpg

All 101 actions are grouped into five types of actions as follows: Human-object interaction, Body motion, Human-human interaction, Playing musical instruments, and Sports. The dataset and annotation can be downloaded from `http://crcv.ucf.edu/data/UCF101.php`.

Next, we will learn about the YouTube-8M dataset.

YouTube-8M

The **YouTube-8M** dataset is for video classification problems. The dataset contains video URLs with labels and visual features. Here are a few statistics about the dataset:

- **Number of video URLs**: 7 million
- **Hours of video clips**: 450,000
- **Number of class labels**: 4,716
- **Average number of labels per video**: 3.4

Here is the summary of the dataset, across various genres:

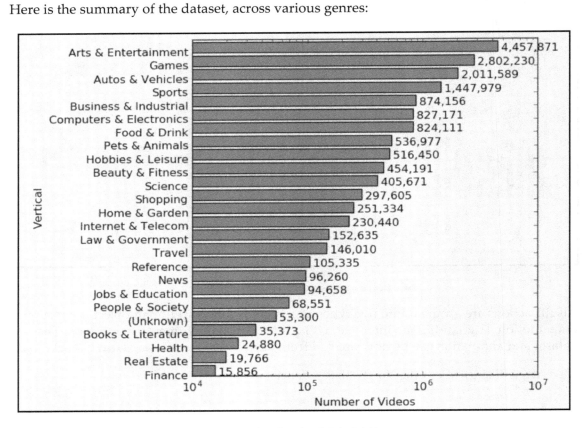

Source: https://research.google.com/youtube8m/vertical-videos.png

The preceding image can give a glimpse of the type of labels available in the dataset. The video data is large and hence visual features are computed and provided with the dataset. The dataset can be accessed through this link: `https://research.google.com/youtube8m/`.

Other datasets

There are some more datasets available for video classification problems. Here are the details of a few more datasets:

- **Sports-1M (Sports - 1 Million)**: Has 1,133,158 videos with 487 classes. The annotations are done automatically. The dataset can be downloaded from: `http://cs.stanford.edu/people/karpathy/deepvideo/`.
- **UCF-11 (University of Central Florida - 11 actions)**: Has 1,600 videos with 11 actions. The videos have 29.97 fps (frames per second). The dataset can be downloaded along with `UCF101`.
- **HMDB-51 (Human Motion DataBase - 51 actions)**: Has 5,100 videos with 51 actions. The dataset link is: `http://serre-lab.clps.brown.edu/resource/hmdb-a-large-human-motion-database`.
- **Hollywood2**: Has 1,707 videos with 12 actions. The dataset link is: `http://www.di.ens.fr/~laptev/actions/hollywood2`.

We have seen the datasets available for video classification tasks, along with the description and access links. Next, we will see how to load a video and split it into frames for further processing.

Splitting videos into frames

A video can be converted to frames and saved in a directory for further usage. Splitting into frames helps us save time by decompressing the video before the training process. First, let's see a code snippet for converting video to frames:

```
import cv2
video_handle = cv2.VideoCapture(video_path)
frame_no = 0
while True:
  eof, frame = video_handle.read()
  if not eof:
      break
  cv2.imwrite("frame%d.jpg" % frame_no, frame)
  frame_no += 1
```

Using this snippet, all of the preceding datasets can be converted to frames. Note that this will require a lot of hard disk space.

Approaches for classifying videos

Videos have to be classified for several applications. Since the video is a lot of data, training and inference computations must also be accounted for. All video classification approaches are inspired by image classification algorithms. The standard architectures such as VGG, Inception, and so on are used for feature computation at a frame level and then processed further. Concepts such as **CNN**, **attention**, and **LSTM** learned in previous chapters will be useful here. Intuitively, the following approaches can be used for video classification:

- Extract the frames and use the models learned in Chapter 2, *Image Classification,* for classification on a frame basis.
- Extract the image features learned in Chapter 3, *Image Retrieval,* and the features can be used train an RNN as described in Chapter 7, *Image Captioning.*
- Train a **3D convolution** network on the whole video. 3D convolution is an extension of 2D convolution; we will see the workings of 3D convolution in detail in the following sections.
- Use the **optical flow** of the video to further improve the accuracy. Optical flow is the pattern of movement of objects, which we will see in detail in coming sections.

We will see several algorithms that give good accuracy with various computational complexities. The dataset can be prepared by converting it into frames and subsampling it to the same length. Some preprocessing can help, such as subtracting the mean of the Imagenet.

Fusing parallel CNN for video classification

Frame-wise, the prediction of a video may not yield good results due to the downsampling of images, which loses fine details. Using a high-resolution CNN will increase the inference time. Hence, Karpathy et al. (`https://static.googleusercontent.com/media/research.google.com/en//pubs/archive/42455.pdf`) propose fusing two streams that are run in parallel for video classification. There are two problems with doing frame-wise predictions, namely:

- Predictions may take a long time because of the larger CNN architecture
- Independent predictions lose the information along the temporal dimension

The architecture can be simplified with fewer parameters with two smaller encoders running in parallel. The video is passed simultaneously through two CNN encoders. One encoder takes a low resolution and processes high resolution. The encoder has alternating convolution, normalization, and pooling layers. The final layer of the two encoders is connected through the fully connected layer. The other encoder is of the same size, but takes only the central crop, as shown here:

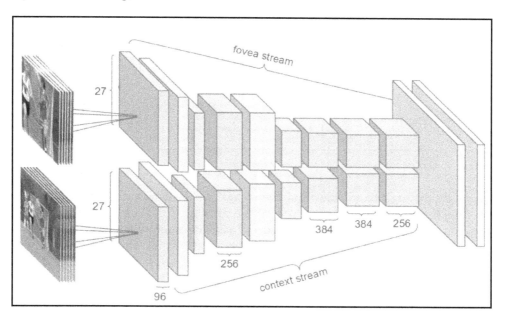

Reproduced from Karpathy et al.

Parallel processing of frames makes the runtime faster by downsampling the video. The CNN architecture is halved regarding the parameter while maintaining the same accuracy. The two streams are called the **fovea** and **context** streams. The streams are shown in the following code snippet:

```
high_resolution_input = tf.placeholder(tf.float32, shape=[None,
input_size])
low_resolution_input = tf.placeholder(tf.float32, shape=[None, input_size])
y_input = tf.placeholder(tf.float32, shape=[None, no_classes])
high_resolution_cnn = get_model(high_resolution_input)
low_resolution_cnn = get_model(low_resolution_input)
dense_layer_1 = tf.concat([high_resolution_cnn, low_resolution_cnn], 1)
dense_layer_bottleneck = dense_layer(dense_layer_1, 1024)
logits = dense_layer(dense_layer_bottleneck, no_classes)
```

The frames for processing across temporal dimensions are as shown in the following diagram:

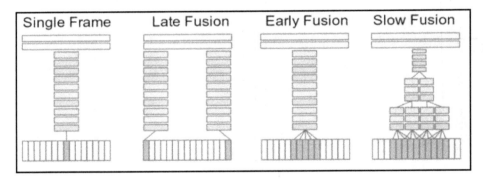

Reproduced from Karpathy et al.

Instead of going through fixed size clips, the video can be seen at different times. Three ways of connecting the temporal information are presented in the preceding image. Late fusion requires a longer time frame while early fusion sees a few frames together. Slow fusion combines both late and early fusion to give good results. The model was trained on the Sports1M dataset, which has 487 classes and achieved an accuracy of 50%. The same model, when applied to UCF101, achieves an accuracy of 60%.

Classifying videos over long periods

The fusion method works well for short video snippets. Classifying longer videos is difficult as a lot of frames have to be computed and remembered. Ng et al. (`https://www.cv-foundation.org/openaccess/content_cvpr_2015/papers/Ng_Beyond_Short_Snippets_2015_CVPR_paper.pdf`) proposed two methods for classifying longer videos:

- The first approach is to pool the convolutional features temporally. Max-pooling is used as a feature `aggregation` method.
- The second approach has an LSTM connecting the convolutional features that handle the variable length of the video.

Both approaches are shown in the following image:

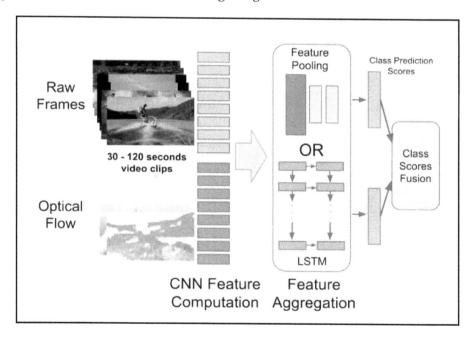

Reproduced from Ng et al.

The CNN features can be extracted and fed to a small LSTM network, as demonstrated in the following code:

```
net = tf.keras.models.Sequential()
net.add(tf.keras.layers.LSTM(2048,
         return_sequences=False,
         input_shape=input_shape,
         dropout=0.5))
net.add(tf.keras.layers.Dense(512, activation='relu'))
net.add(tf.keras.layers.Dropout(0.5))
net.add(tf.keras.layers.Dense(no_classes, activation='softmax'))
```

Adding LSTM for feature pooling instead provides better performance. The features are pooled in various ways, as shown in the following image:

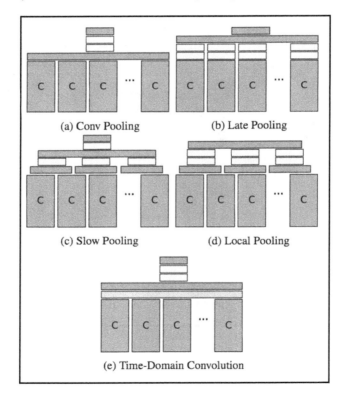

Reproduced from Ng et al.

As shown in the diagram, the convolutional features can be aggregated in several different ways. The pooling is done after the fully connected layer before it. This method achieved an accuracy of 73.1% and 88.6% in the `Sports1M` dataset and `UCF101` datasets respectively. The LSTM approach is shown in the following image:

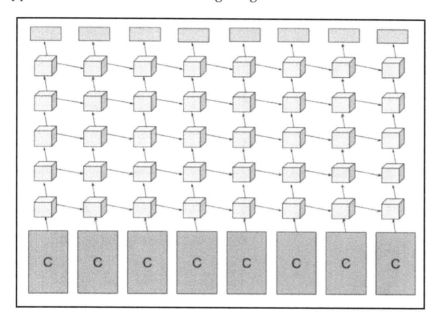

Reproduced from Ng et al.

The computations are high for this model because several LSTM's are used.

Streaming two CNN's for action recognition

The motion of objects in videos has very good information about the actions performed in the video. The motion of objects can be quantified by optical flow. Simonyan and Zisserman (`http://papers.nips.cc/paper/5353-two-stream-convolutional-networks-for-action-recognition-in-videos.pdf`) proposed a method for action recognition that uses two streams from images and optical flow.

Optical flow measures the motion by quantifying the relative movement between the observer and scene. A detailed lecture on optical flow can be found at `https://www.youtube.com/watch?v=5VyLAH8BhF8`. The optical flow can be obtained by running the following command:

```
p1, st, err = cv2.calcOpticalFlowPyrLK(old_gray, frame_gray, p0, None,
**lk_params)
```

One stream takes an individual frame and predicts actions using a regular CNN. The other stream takes multiple frames and computes the optical flow. The optical flow is passed through a CNN for a prediction. Both the predictions are shown in the following image:

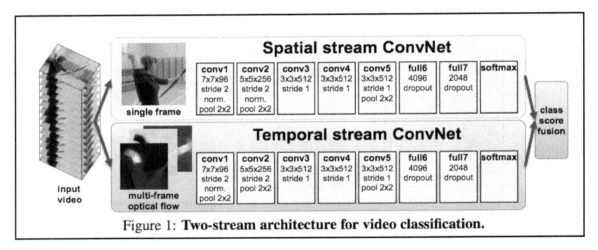

Figure 1: **Two-stream architecture for video classification.**

Both predictions can be combined with the final prediction.

Using 3D convolution for temporal learning

A video can be classified with 3D convolution. 3D convolution operation takes a volume as input and outputs the same, whereas a 2D convolution can take a 2D or volume output and outputs a 2D image. The difference is shown as follows:

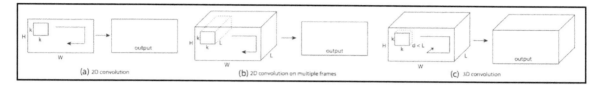

The first two images belong to 2D convolution. The output is always an image. 3D convolution, meanwhile, outputs a volume. The difference is a convolution operation in 3 directions with the kernel. Tran et al. (`https://www.cv-foundation.org/openaccess/content_iccv_2015/papers/Tran_Learning_Spatiotemporal_Features_ICCV_2015_paper.pdf`) used 3D convolution for video classification. The 3D convolution model is shown as follows:

The following is a code snippet of the model using 3D convolution:

```
net = tf.keras.models.Sequential()
net.add(tf.keras.layers.Conv3D(32,
                               kernel_size=(3, 3, 3),
                               input_shape=(input_shape)))
net.add(tf.keras.layers.Activation('relu'))
net.add(tf.keras.layers.Conv3D(32, (3, 3, 3)))
net.add(tf.keras.layers.Activation('softmax'))
net.add(tf.keras.layers.MaxPooling3D())
net.add(tf.keras.layers.Dropout(0.25))

net.add(tf.keras.layers.Conv3D(64, (3, 3, 3)))
net.add(tf.keras.layers.Activation('relu'))
net.add(tf.keras.layers.Conv3D(64, (3, 3, 3)))
net.add(tf.keras.layers.Activation('softmax'))
net.add(tf.keras.layers.MaxPool3D())
```

```
net.add(tf.keras.layers.Dropout(0.25))

net.add(tf.keras.layers.Flatten())
net.add(tf.keras.layers.Dense(512, activation='sigmoid'))
net.add(tf.keras.layers.Dropout(0.5))
net.add(tf.keras.layers.Dense(no_classes, activation='softmax'))
net.compile(loss=tf.keras.losses.categorical_crossentropy,
            optimizer=tf.keras.optimizers.Adam(), metrics=['accuracy'])
```

 3D convolution needs a lot of computing power. 3D convolution achieves an accuracy of 90.2% on the `Sports1M` dataset.

Using trajectory for classification

Wang et al. (`https://www.cv-foundation.org/openaccess/content_cvpr_2015/papers/Wang_Action_Recognition_With_2015_CVPR_paper.pdf`) used the trajectory of parts of bodies to classify the actions performed. This work combines handcrafted and deep learned features for final predictions. The following is a representation of the classification:

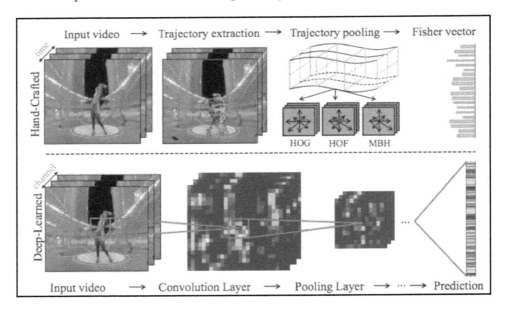

Reproduced from Wang et al.

The handcrafted features are **Fisher vector** and the features are from CNN. The following image demonstrates the extraction of the trajectories and features maps:

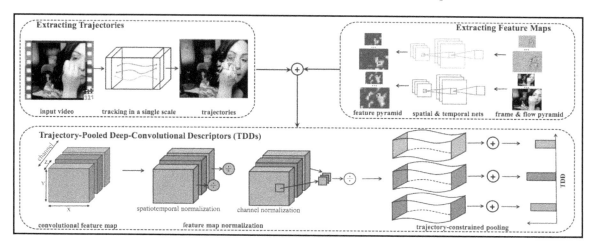

Reproduced from Wang et al.

Both the trajectories and features maps are combined temporally to form the final predictions over the temporal snippet.

Multi-modal fusion

Yang et al. (`http://research.nvidia.com/sites/default/files/pubs/2016-10_Multilayer-and-Multimodal/MM16.pdf`) proposed a multi-modal fusion, with 4 models, for video classification. The four models are 3D convolution features, 2D optical flow, 3D optical flow, and 2D convolution features.

The flow of data in this method is shown as follows:

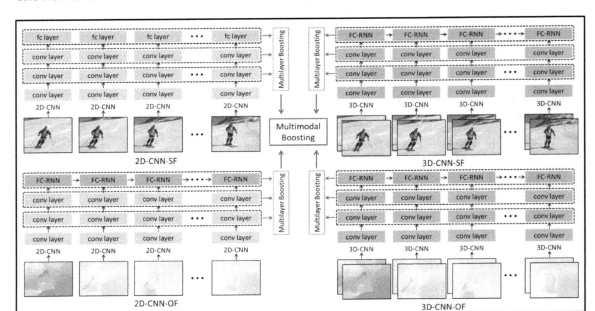

Now, let's learn about **Convlet**. A **Convlet** is the small convolutional output from a single kernel. The learning of spatial weights in the convolution layer by **convlet** is shown in the following image:

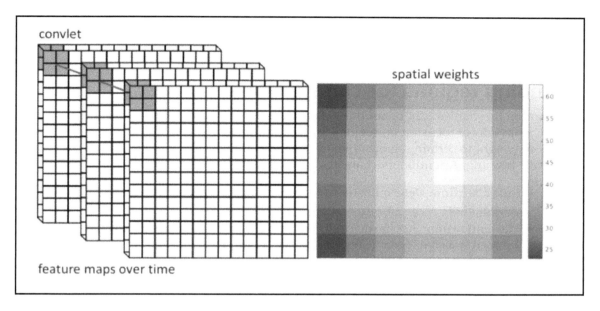

A spatial weight indicates how discriminative or important a local spatial region is in a convolutional layer. The following image is an illustration of fusing multi-layer representation, done at various layers of convolutional and fully connected layers:

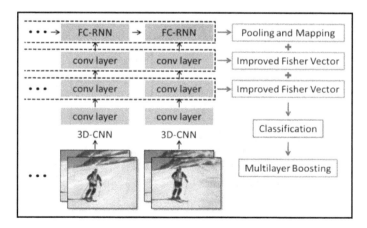

The boosting mechanism is used to combine the predictions. **Boosting** is a mechanism that can combine several model prediction into a final prediction.

Attending regions for classification

An attention mechanism can be used for classification. Attention mechanisms replicate the human behaviour of focusing on regions for recognition activities. Attention mechanisms give more weight to certain regions than others. The method of weight is learned from the data while training. Attention mechanisms are mainly of two types, namely:

- **Soft attention**: Deterministic in character, this can hence be learned by back-propagation.
- **Hard attention**: Stochastic in character, this needs complicated mechanisms to learn. It is also expensive because of the requirement of sampling data.

Following is a visualization of soft attention:

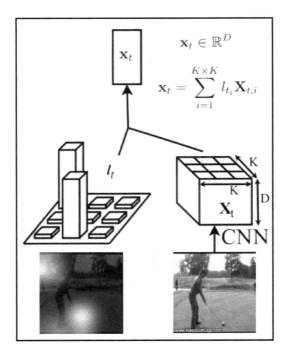

Reproduced from Sharma et al.

The **CNN** features are computed and weighted according to the attention. The attention or weights given to certain areas can be used for visualization. Sharma et al. (`https://arxiv.org/pdf/1511.04119.pdf`) used this idea to classify the videos. **LSTM** were used to take the convolution features. The **LSTM** predicts the regions by using attention on following frames, as shown in the following image:

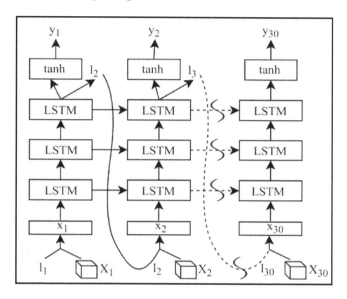

Reproduced from Sharma et al.

Each stack of **LSTM** predicts location and labels. Every stack has three **LSTM**. The input to the **LSTM** stack is a convolution feature cube and location. The location probabilities are the attention weights. The use of attention gives an improvement in accuracy as well as a method to visualize the predictions.

We have seen various approaches for video classification. Next, we will learn about other applications in videos.

Extending image-based approaches to videos

Images can be used for pose estimation, style transfer, image generation, segmentation, captioning, and so on. Similarly, these applications find a place in videos too. Using the temporal information may improve the predictions from images and vice versa. In this section, we will see how to extend these applications to videos.

Regressing the human pose

Human pose estimation is an important application of video data and can improve other tasks such as action recognition. First, let's see a description of the datasets available for pose estimation:

- **Poses in the wild dataset**: Contains 30 videos annotated with the human pose. The dataset link is: `https://lear.inrialpes.fr/research/posesinthewild/`. The dataset is annotated with human upper body joints.
- **Frames Labeled In Cinema (FLIC)**: A human pose dataset obtained from 30 movies, available at: `https://bensapp.github.io/flic-dataset.html`.

Pfister et al. (`https://www.cv-foundation.org/openaccess/content_iccv_2015/papers/Pfister_Flowing_ConvNets_for_ICCV_2015_paper.pdf`) proposed a method to predict the human pose in videos. The following is the pipeline for regressing the human pose:

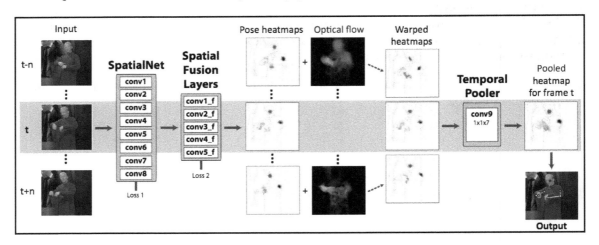

Reproduced from Pfister et al.

The frames from the video are taken and passed through a convolutional network. The layers are fused, and the pose heatmaps are obtained. The pose heatmaps are combined with optical flow to get the warped heatmaps. The warped heatmaps across a timeframe are pooled to produce the pooled heatmap, getting the final pose.

Tracking facial landmarks

Face analysis in videos requires face detection, landmark detection, pose estimation, verification, and so on. Computing landmarks are especially crucial for capturing facial animation, human-computer interaction, and human activity recognition. Instead of computing over frames, it can be computed over video. Gu et al. (`http://research.nvidia.com/sites/default/files/pubs/2017-07_Dynamic-Facial-Analysis/rnnface.pdf`) proposed a method to use a joint estimation of detection and tracking of facial landmarks in videos using RNN. The results outperform frame wise predictions and other previous models. The landmarks are computed by CNN, and the temporal aspect is encoded in an RNN. Synthetic data was used for training.

Segmenting videos

Videos can be segmented in a better way when temporal information is used. Gadde et al. (`https://ps.is.tuebingen.mpg.de/uploads_file/attachment/attachment/386/gadde2017videocnns.pdf`) proposed a method to combine temporal information by warping. The following image demonstrates the solution, which segments two frames and combines the warping:

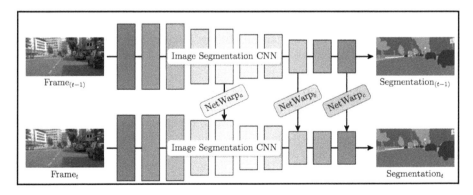

Reproduced from Gadde et al.

The warping net is shown in the following image:

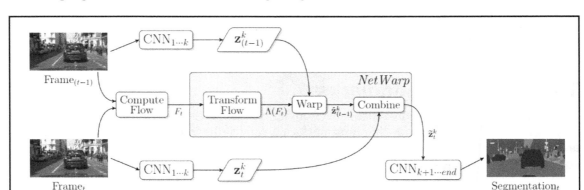

Reproduced from Gadde et al.

The optical flow is computed between two frames, which are combined with warping. The warping module takes the optical flow, transforms it, and combines it with the warped representations.

Captioning videos

The `Chapter 7`, *Image Captioning*, illustrated several ways to combine text and image. Similarly, captions can be generated for videos, describing the context. Let's see a list of the datasets available for captioning videos:

- **Microsoft Research - Video To Text** (**MSR-VTT**) has 200,000 video clip and sentence pairs. More details can be obtained from: `https://www.microsoft.com/en-us/research/publication/msr-vtt-a-large-video-description-dataset-for-bridging-video-and-language/`.
- **MPII Movie Description Corpus** (**MPII-MD**) can be obtained from: `https://www.mpi-inf.mpg.de/departments/computer-vision-and-multimodal-computing/research/vision-and-language/mpii-movie-description-dataset`. It has 68,000 sentences with 94 movies.

- **Montreal Video Annotation Dataset** (**M-VAD**) can be obtained from: `https://mila.quebec/en/publications/public-datasets/m-vad/` and has 49,000 clips.
- **YouTube2Text** has 1,970 videos with 80,000 descriptions.

Yao et al. (`https://www.cv-foundation.org/openaccess/content_iccv_2015/papers/Yao_Describing_Videos_by_ICCV_2015_paper.pdf`) proposed a method for captioning videos. A 3D convolutional network trained for action recognition is used to extract the local temporal features. An attention mechanism is then used on the features to generate text using an RNN. The process is shown here:

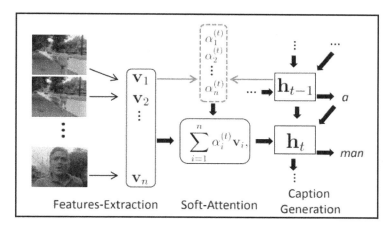

Reproduced from Yao et al.

Donahue et al. (`https://www.cv-foundation.org/openaccess/content_cvpr_2015/papers/Donahue_Long-Term_Recurrent_Convolutional_2015_CVPR_paper.pdf`) proposed another method for video captioning or description, which uses **LSTM** with convolution features.

This is similar to the preceding approach, except that we use 2D convolution features over here, as shown in the following image:

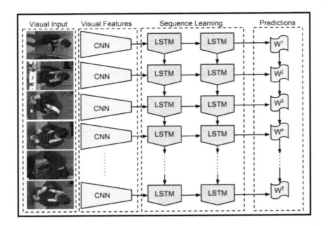

Reproduced from Donahue et al.

We have several ways to combine text with images, such as activity recognition, image description, and video description techniques. The following image illustrates these techniques:

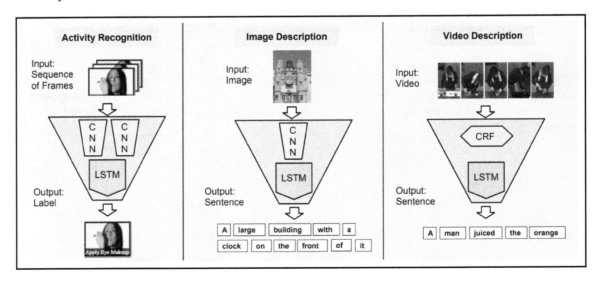

Reproduced from Donahue et al.

Venugopalan et al. (`https://www.cv-foundation.org/openaccess/content_iccv_2015/papers/Venugopalan_Sequence_to_Sequence_ICCV_2015_paper.pdf`) proposed a method for video captioning using an encoder-decoder approach. The following is a visualization of the technique proposed by him:

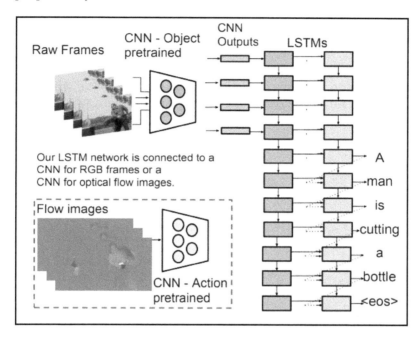

Reproduced from Venugopalan et al.

The **CNN** can be computed on the frames or the optical flow of the images for this method.

Generating videos

Videos can be generated using generative models, in an unsupervised manner. The future frames can be predicted using the current frame. Ranzato et al. (`https://arxiv.org/pdf/1412.6604.pdf`) proposed a method for generating videos, inspired by language models. An RNN model is utilized to take a patch of the image and predict the next patch.

Summary

In this chapter, we covered various topics related to video classification. We saw how to split videos into frames and use the deep learning models that are in images for various tasks. We covered a few algorithms that are specific to video, such as tracking objects. We saw how to apply video-based solutions to various scenarios such as action recognition, gesture recognition, security applications, and intrusion detection.

In the next chapter, we will learn how to deploy the trained models from the previous chapter into production on various cloud and mobile platforms. We will see how different hardware affects the performance regarding latency and throughput.

10
Deployment

In this chapter, we will learn how to deploy the trained model in the various platforms for maximum throughput and minimum latency. We will understand performance on various hardware such as a GPU and a CPU. We will follow the steps of deploying TensorFlow in platforms such as Amazon Web Services, Google Cloud Platform, and mobile platforms such as Android, iOS, and Tegra.

We will cover the following topics in this chapter:

- Understanding the factors affecting the performance of the deep learning model training and inference
- Improving the performance through various methods
- Seeing the benchmarks of various hardware and learning the steps to tweak them for maximum performance
- Using various cloud platforms for deployment
- Using various mobile platforms for deployment

Performance of models

Performance is important for both the training and the deployment of deep learning models. The training usually takes more time due to large data or big model architecture. The resultant models may be a bigger size and hence problematic to use in mobile devices where there is a constraint on RAM. More computing time results in more infrastructure cost. The inference time is critical in video applications. Due to the previously mentioned importance of performance, in this section, we will look at techniques to improve the performance. Reducing the model complexity is an easy option but results in decreasing accuracy. Here, we will focus on methods to improve the performance with an insignificant drop in accuracy. In the next section, we will discuss the option of quantization.

Quantizing the models

The weights of deep learning models have 32-bit float values. When the weights are quantized to 8-bit, the decrease in accuracy is small and hence cannot be noticed in deployment. The precision of weights on the results seems to have fewer effects on accuracy performance of deep learning models. This idea is interesting about deep learning and useful when the model size becomes critical. By replacing 32-bit float values with 8-bit values, the model size can be significantly decreased and the inference speed can be increased. There are plenty of options when implementing the quantization of models. The weights can be stored in 8-bit but inference operations can be performed in 32-bit float values. Every component of the architecture may behave differently for quantization size and so, depending on the layer, 32 or 16 or 8-bit values can be chosen.

The quantization works due to a number of reasons. Generally, the deep learning models are trained to tackle noise in the images and therefore can be considered as robust. The inference calculations can have redundant information and that redundant information may be removed due to the quantization.

The latest CPU and RAM hardware are tuned towards floating point calculation and so the effect of quantization may be less visible in such hardware. This scenario is changing as more and more hardware is introduced for this purpose. A significant difference in memory and speed can be noticed in GPUs as they are now adapted to the lower precise floating operations. There is other special hardware available for running less precise floating operations.

MobileNets

Howard and others (https://arxiv.org/pdf/1704.04861.pdf) introduced a new class of models called **MobileNets** that can be used for mobile and embedded applications. MobileNets can be used for different applications such as object detection, landmark recognition, face attributes, fine-grain classification as shown here:

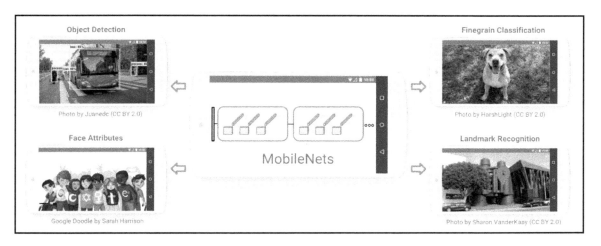

MobileNets reduced the size and computation of models by replacing standard convolution filters (**a**) with depthwise (**b**) and pointwise convolutions (**c**) as shown here:

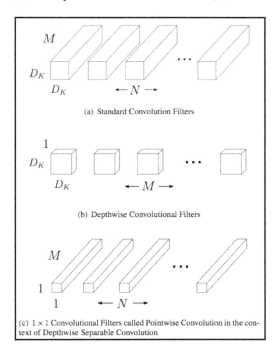

(a) Standard Convolution Filters

(b) Depthwise Convolutional Filters

(c) 1×1 Convolutional Filters called Pointwise Convolution in the context of Depthwise Separable Convolution

The batch normalization and activation layers are added to both depthwise and pointwise convolutions as shown here:

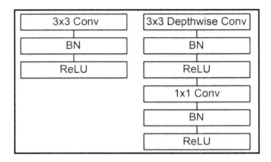

Reproduced from Howard and others

There are two parameters affecting the choice of models:

- **The number of multiplication and additions**: The trade-off between accuracy and mult-adds is shown below:

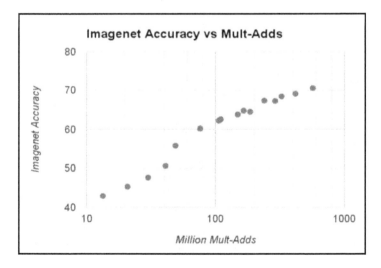

Reproduced from Howard and others

- **The number of parameters in the model**: The trade-off is shown here:

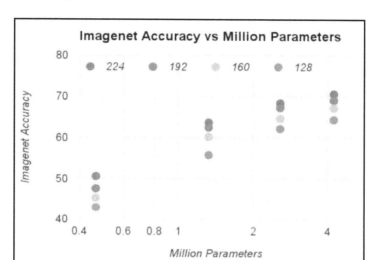

Reproduced from Howard and others

MobileNets has shown that model computation and size can be reduced with a small reduction in accuracy to be used on mobile and embedded devices. The exact trade-offs between models and accuracies can be seen in the article by Howard and others.

Deployment in the cloud

The models have to be deployed in the cloud for several applications. We will look at major cloud service providers for this purpose.

AWS

The Amazon Web Services (AWS) extends support to the development and deployment of TensorFlow-based models. Sign up for AWS at `https://aws.amazon.com/` and select one of the **Amazon Machine Images (AMI)**. AMIs are images of machines with all the required software installed. You need not worry about installing the packages. **AWS provides Deep Learning AMI (DLAMI)** for ease of training and deploying deep learning models. There are several options to choose from. Here, we will use Conda as it comes with several packages required for running TensorFlow. There are two options for Python: version 2 and 3. The following code will activate TensorFlow with Keras 2 on Python 3 on CUDA 8:

```
source activate tensorflow_p36
```

The following code will activate TensorFlow with Keras 2 on Python 2 on CUDA 8:

```
source activate tensorflow_p27
```

 You can visit `https://aws.amazon.com/tensorflow/` for more details and tutorials.

A **Virtual Machine (VM)** can also be started by following the steps given here:

1. Go to `aws.amazon.com` and login using your Amazon account.
2. Choose **Launch a virtual machine** from the login page:

Build a solution

Get started with simple wizards and automated workflows.

Launch a virtual machine	Build a web app	Host a static website
With EC2 or Lightsail	With Elastic Beanstalk	With S3, CloudFront, Route 53
~1-2 minutes	~6 minutes	~5 minutes

Connect an IoT device	Start a development project	Register a domain
With AWS IoT	With CodeStar	With Route 53
~5 minutes	~5 minutes	~3 minutes

3. In the next window, choose the **EC2 Instance** by clicking on **Get Started** as shown here:

 EC2 Instance

For users with cloud experience who need a
flexible and scalable virtual machine*

Why EC2 ?

- Fully customizable instance tailored to your needs.
- Seamless integration with AWS services.
- Flexible solution that scales to support changing workloads.

Pricing

- Pay as you go. Learn more
- Free-tier eligible. Learn more

Get started

*This wizard creates an EC2 t2.micro instance with default configurations. For more
options, use the EC2 launch instance wizard.

4. Give a name to the **EC2 Instance**:

5. Select the type of **Operating System**:

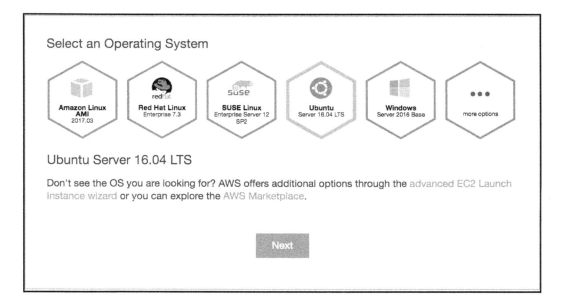

6. Select the **instance** type. The instance types indicated the type of configurations with varying sizes of RAM and CPU. There are a couple of options to select from GPU's as well. Choose the instance type and click 'Next' button:

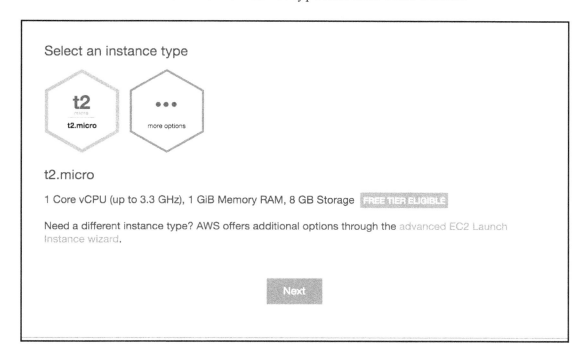

7. Create a Privacy Enhanced Mail Security Certificate (PEM) file that will be used for logging in as shown here:

Create a key pair

Amazon EC2 secures your instance using a key pair. In this step you will download the private key to your computer.

Save it in a safe place and use it when you connect to your instance.

tensorflow

8. It will take some time to create the instance and at the end, a completed status will be shown:

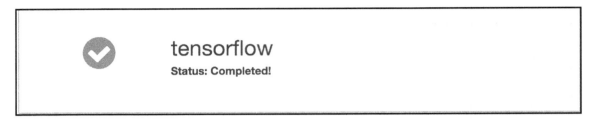

9. Next, click on the **Proceed to EC2 console** button:

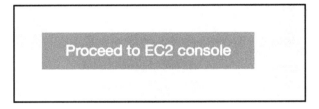

10. Now the instance will be created; click on the **Connect** button as shown here:

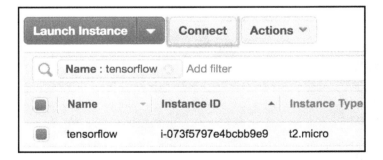

11. Next, the instance has to be connected to a command prompt of the virtual machine. The instructions required to connect are given in this step. You will need the 'pem' file downloaded in the previous steps. Follow the instructions displayed to connect to the system:

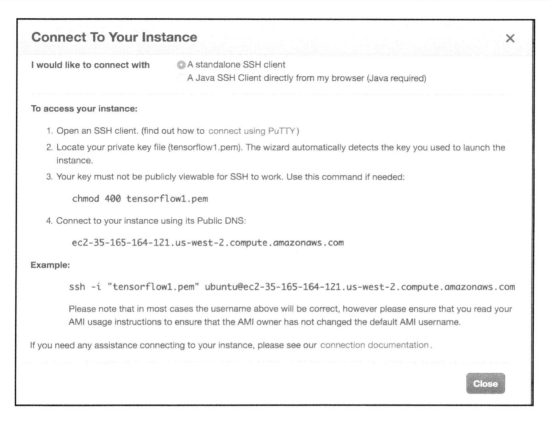

Connect To Your Instance   ×

I would like to connect with   ⦿ A standalone SSH client
         ○ A Java SSH Client directly from my browser (Java required)

To access your instance:

1. Open an SSH client. (find out how to connect using PuTTY)

2. Locate your private key file (tensorflow1.pem). The wizard automatically detects the key you used to launch the instance.

3. Your key must not be publicly viewable for SSH to work. Use this command if needed:

    ```
    chmod 400 tensorflow1.pem
    ```

4. Connect to your instance using its Public DNS:

    ```
    ec2-35-165-164-121.us-west-2.compute.amazonaws.com
    ```

Example:

```
ssh -i "tensorflow1.pem" ubuntu@ec2-35-165-164-121.us-west-2.compute.amazonaws.com
```

Please note that in most cases the username above will be correct, however please ensure that you read your AMI usage instructions to ensure that the AMI owner has not changed the default AMI username.

If you need any assistance connecting to your instance, please see our connection documentation.

     Close

12. Once you are done, terminate the instance by clicking **Actions | Instance State | Terminate:**

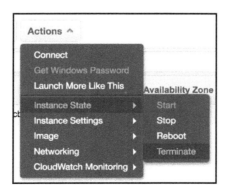

The installation and execution steps can be followed by `Chapter 1`, *Getting Started.*

Google Cloud Platform

Google Cloud Platform (GCP) is the cloud platform offered by Google and has similar functionalities of AWS. A simple Virtual Machine can be utilized for training the models like AWS, by following these steps:

1. Go to the Google Cloud Platform using `cloud.google.com` and log in to the platform using your Gmail account.
2. Now proceed to the console by clicking the **GO TO CONSOLE** button:

3. After proceeding to the console, move to the **VM creation page** by clicking **Compute Engine** | **VM instances** from the top-right hand side menu, as shown in the following screenshot:

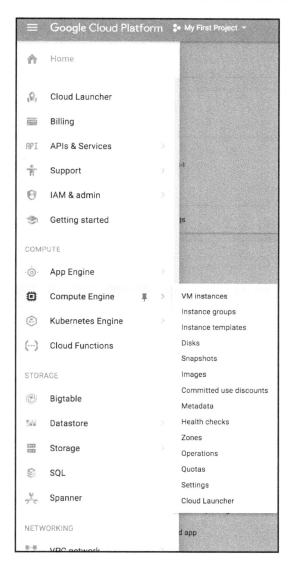

4. Then click on the **CREATE INSTANCE** button, in order to create the required instance:

5. Next, the instance type can be selected with the configurations. Zone parameter informs the region the instance will be deployed. By selecting the zone close to the users, one can save latency time. The machine type can be customized with required RAM and CPU's. GPU's also can be selected for faster training. Select the size of the instance and click 'Create' button, as shown in the following screenshot:

6. It will take a few minutes to create the instance. Then click on the **SSH** drop-down list for the instance and select 'Open in browser window' option, as shown here to open the console in the browser:

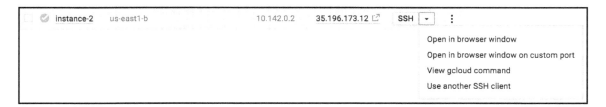

Using the shell, you can install TensorFlow and can train or deploy models. There are a lot of options available to choose from the configuration of virtual machines. Depending upon the cost and time tradeoff, one can choose the configurations.

The GCP has a **Cloud Machine Learning Engine** that helps us while using TensorFlow. There are three components of GCP that can be utilized together for architecting a training and deployment infrastructure:

1. Cloud DataFlow for preprocessing the images
2. Cloud Machine Learning Engine for both training and deploying a model
3. Google Cloud Storage for storing training data, code and results

An excellent tutorial to build a customized image classification model using the Cloud Machine Learning Engine can be found at `https:/` `/cloud.google.com/ml-engine/docs/flowers-tutorial`.

Deployment of models in devices

TensorFlow models can be deployed in mobile devices too. Mobile devices include smartphones, drones, home robots and so on. Billions of smartphones can have applications of computer vision which can use deep learning. One can take a photo and search, stream a video with scenes tagged and so on. Deploying in mobile devices means that the deep learning model is present on the device and inference happens on the device. Models deployed on the device helps in privacy issues. In the following topics, we will discuss how to deploy them across various mobile platforms.

Jetson TX2

Jetson TX2 is an embedding device supplied by NVIDIA specifically efficient AI computing. Jetson TX2 is lightweight, compact and hence suitable for deployment in drones, public places and so on. It also ships preinstalled TensorRT which is a runtime for TensorFlow. You can buy Jetson and flash install Ubuntu, CUDA, CUDNN before installing TensorFlow. Clone `https://github.com/jetsonhacks/installTensorFlowTX2` and enter the following commands at the command prompt.

1. First, install the prerequisites with the help of the following code:

   ```
   ./installPrerequisites.sh
   ```

2. Now, clone the TensorFlow using the following code:

   ```
   ./cloneTensorFlow.sh
   ```

3. Next, set the required environment variables using the following code:

   ```
   ./setTensorFlowEV.sh
   ```

4. Now we will build the TensorFlow using the following code:

   ```
   ./buildTensorFlow.sh
   ```

5. Now we will process the package into a wheel file using the following code:

   ```
   ./packageTensorFlow.sh
   ```

6. Now we will install the Tensorflow using the following code:

   ```
   pip install $HOME/tensorflow-1.0.1-cp27-cp27mu-linux_aarch64.whl
   ```

With the help of these steps, we can install TensorFlow in Jetson TX2.

Android

Any Android app can use TensorFlow and the details to build can be found in `https://www.tensorflow.org/mobile/android_build`. The official example regarding this can be found in `https://github.com/tensorflow/tensorflow/tree/master/tensorflow/examples/android`. The steps for implementing Tensorflow in Android devices are as follows assuming the reader has experience in Android programming:

1. Export the TensorFlow model to a `.pb` file using the steps covered in `Chapter 3`, *Image Retrieval*.
2. Build `.so` and `.jar` files which are the binaries.
3. Edit `gradle` files to enable loading of libraries.
4. Load and run the Android app file

iPhone

Apple used CoreML framework to integrate machine learning in the applications of iPhone. Apple provides a standard list of models that can be integrated directly into the application. You can train a custom deep learning models using TensorFlow and use that in iPhone. In order to deploy custom models, you have to covert the TensorFlow in CoreML framework model. Google released `https://github.com/tf-coreml/tf-coreml` for converting TensorFlow models into CoreML models. TFcoreML can be installed using the following code:

```
pip install -U tfcoreml
```

The model can be exported using the following code:

```
import tfcoreml as tf_converter
tf_converter.convert(tf_model_path='tf_model_path.pb',
                     mlmodel_path='mlmodel_path.mlmodel',
                     output_feature_names=['softmax:0'],
                     input_name_shape_dict={'input:0': [1, 227, 227, 3]})
```

The exported model can be used by iPhone for predictions.

Summary

In this chapter, we have seen how to deploy the trained deep learning models on various platforms and devices. We have covered the steps as well as guidelines on getting the best performance for these platforms. We have seen the advantages of MobileNets for reducing the inference time with a small trade-off of accuracy.

Other Books You May Enjoy

If you enjoyed this book, you may be interested in these other books by Packt:

TensorFlow 1.x Deep Learning Cookbook
Antonio Gulli, Amita Kapoor

ISBN: 978-1-78829-359-4

- Install TensorFlow and use it for CPU and GPU operations
- Implement DNNs and apply them to solve different AI-driven problems.
- Leverage different data sets such as MNIST, CIFAR-10, and Youtube8m with TensorFlow and learn how to access and use them in your code.
- Use TensorBoard to understand neural network architectures, optimize the learning process, and peek inside the neural network black box.
- Use different regression techniques for prediction and classification problems
- Build single and multilayer perceptrons in TensorFlow

>

Deep Learning with Keras

Antonio Gulli, Sujit Pal

ISBN: 978-1-78712-842-2

- Optimize step-by-step functions on a large neural network using the Backpropagation Algorithm
- Fine-tune a neural network to improve the quality of results
- Use deep learning for image and audio processing
- Use Recursive Neural Tensor Networks (RNTNs) to outperform standard word embedding in special cases
- Identify problems for which Recurrent Neural Network (RNN) solutions are suitable
- Explore the process required to implement Autoencoders
- Evolve a deep neural network using reinforcement learning

Leave a review - let other readers know what you think

Please share your thoughts on this book with others by leaving a review on the site that you bought it from. If you purchased the book from Amazon, please leave us an honest review on this book's Amazon page. This is vital so that other potential readers can see and use your unbiased opinion to make purchasing decisions, we can understand what our customers think about our products, and our authors can see your feedback on the title that they have worked with Packt to create. It will only take a few minutes of your time, but is valuable to other potential customers, our authors, and Packt. Thank you!

Index

batch normalization 14
blending 212, 213
boosting 256
bottleneck features
    training 73, 74
bottleneck layer 103

C

Canadian Institute for Advanced Research
    (CIFAR) 56
captions
    retrieving, from images 193
characters 184
CIFAR dataset 56, 57
Cloud Machine Learning Engine 279
cloud
    Amazon Web Services (AWS) 270, 272, 275
    deployment 269
    Google Cloud Platform (GCP) 279
CNN features 257
COCO object detection challenge 111
Common Objects in Context (COCO) 111
competition 59
Computed Tomography (CT) 133
Computer Unified Device Architecture (CUDA) 27
conditional GAN 232
conditional random field (CRF) 143
    about 188
    used, for linking image 188
    used, for linking text 188
connected layer
    training, as convolution layer 115
content loss 217, 218, 219, 220, 221
content-based image retrieval (CBIR)
    about 96
    autoencoders, used for image denoising 104
    efficient retrieval 100
    geometric verification 97
    Locality sensitive hashing (LSH) 96
    multi-index hashing 96
    query expansion 97
    relevance feedback 97
    retrieval pipeline, building 97
context streams 246
convolution implementation

of sliding window 116
convolutional neural networks (CNN)
    about 18, 244
    kernel 18
    max pooling 19
cross-entropy 13
CUDA Deep Neural Network (CUDNN)
    about 29
    URL, for downloading 29
CUDA library
    URL, for downloading 28

D

data
    preparing 69, 70
datasets 135
    about 183, 243
    augmentation techniques 72
    augmenting 71
    COCO object detection challenge 111
    evaluating, metrics used 112
    exploring 110
    ImageNet dataset 111
    Intersection over Union (IoU) 112
    mean average precision 113
    PASCAL VOC challenge 111
decoder 103
deconvolution 139
deep learning models
    about 60
    AlexNet model 60
    DenseNet model 67, 68
    Google Inception-V3 model 62, 64, 65
    Microsoft ResNet-50 model 65
    MobileNets 266
    parameters 268
    performance 265
    quantising 266
    spatial transformer networks 67
    SqueezeNet model 65, 66
    VGG-16 model 61
deep learning
    about 7
    activation functions 8
    artificial neural network (ANN) 12

multi-spline method 212
Multi-Task Facial Landmark (MTFL) dataset 170
multilayer convolutional network
  building 44, 45, 46, 47, 48, 49
  TensorBoard, utilizing in deep learning 49, 50, 51, 52, 53
multimodal embedding space 197
multimodal metric space 197

N

Natural Language Processing (NLP) 234
natural language processing (NLP) 25, 184
neural artistic style transfer
  about 216
  content loss 217, 218, 219
neural nets 8

O

object detection API
  about 123
  installing 123
  pedestrian detection, training for self-driving car 128
  pre-trained models 125
  re-training object detection models 126
  setting up 124
object localization 110
objects
  connected layer, training as convolution layer 115
  convolution implementation, of sliding window 116
  detecting 120
  detecting, in an image 109
  Fast R-CNN 121, 122
  localizing, sliding windows used 114
  Regions of the convolutional neural network (R-CNN) 120
  scale-space concept 115
  Single shot multi-box detector 122
one-hot encoding 13
one-shot learning 160
Open Computer Vision (OpenCV)
  about 30
  URL 30

operating systems
  about 27
  General Purpose - Graphics Processing Unit (GP-GPU) 27
optical flow 244
optimization 15

P

PASCAL VOC challenge
  about 111
  URL, for downloading 111
pedestrain detection
  training, for self-driving car 128
perceptron
  about 8
  building 41
  model, training with data 43, 44
  placeholders, defining for input data 41, 42
  placeholders, defining for targets 41, 42
  variables, defining for connected layer 42, 43
pip3 30
pixels
  medical images, diagnosing 133
  predicting 131, 132, 133
  robots, enabling 134
  satellite imagery 134
pose detection 117
preprocess function 218
principal component analysis (PCA) 58, 80
Protocol Buffers (protobuf) 123
PSPnet 146
Python 29

R

random noise 218
re-training object detection models
  about 126
  data preparation, for Pet dataset 126
  loss and accuracy monitoring, TensorBoard used 128
  model, training 127
  object detection training pipeline 126
real-world applications
  age detection, from face 78

www.ingramcontent.com/pod-product-compliance
Lightning Source LLC
Chambersburg PA
CBHW080626060326
40690CB00021B/4826